Once upon a time . . .   he
Change seemed to imply   l
being, that potency had le   ld
woman – with no happy e

Then, women such as Germaine Greer (love or loathe her views), brought the menopause out of hiding. Today, an increasing number of women are choosing to celebrate their freedom to be themselves now that their childbearing years are over.

In this sparkling collection of writings, commissioned and introduced by Joanna Goldsworthy, the creative aspects of the menopause are explored with wit and imagination by Doreen Asso, Deirdre Bair, Sara Banerji, Elizabeth Buchan, Janet Burroway, Virginia Browne, Ruth Fainlight, Penelope Farmer, Eva Figes, Margaret Forster, Phyllida Law, Sheila MacLeod, Sara Maitland, Sue O'Sullivan, Ursula Owen, Molly Parkin and Kathleen Rowntree.

Joanna Goldsworthy was born in 1941 in Redhill, Surrey. She spent twenty-seven years at Victor Gollancz Ltd, working first as Victor Gollancz's secretary, later as an editor. She now works part-time as an editor at Doubleday, and freelances the rest of the time. She lives in London.

A Certain Age

Reflecting on the Menopause

Edited by
Joanna Goldsworthy

Published by VIRAGO PRESS Limited May 1993
20–23 Mandela Street, Camden Town, London NW1 0HQ

A CIP catalogue record for this book is available
from the British Library

Printed in Great Britain by
Cox & Wyman Ltd, Reading, Berkshire

For my mother

CONTENTS

Acknowledgements

I would like to thank the contributors to this book, whose willingness to share their feelings with an astounding honesty has made this collection the life-affirming and powerful work that it is; Lennie Goodings, who not only thought of the idea for this book but gave the job of editing it to me, at a time when I most needed that support; Ruth Petrie, who has shown me what an editor can be; and, finally, Percy Sher, a New Man if ever there was one.

THE EGG MOTHER
Ruth Fainlight

In the same soothing tone the god uses
before he mounts her, she whispers
secrets that the stars and trees have told her
against the bird's warm neck
then grips him firmly around feathery sides.

His strong wings raise them high above the coast.
and follow the river's trail
glinting up the valley to its mountain
source. Brought on the backs
of their oracular birds to a rock-strewn field

below the summit-line, sibyls gather:
the Delphic and the Persian,
Cumaean, Erythraean, Tiburtine,
and those from even further –
sudden green oases, weed-fringed islands.

As if it were the Orphic World Egg,
a silver moon floats up
to signal her arrival, and all the women
turn to watch the bird
settle, and catch her first words and smiles.

Using the same tones their gods do,
gentling them into submission,
she strengthens her sisters for their stern duties.
She is the oldest now.
Her time has come to be the Egg Mother.

From Twelve Sibyls

Joshua Sher

INTRODUCTION
Joanna Goldsworthy

I'm amused by my mother's attitude to the ageing of my body. Now in her mid-seventies, she takes it as a personal affront that I should grow older, especially that I should be menopausal – presumably because it makes *her* older – and her response reminds me of the way in which, when I was a teenager, she would flirt with my boyfriends. Even now, she and I are mistaken for sisters. But if I think about it, I can understand her feelings: the only time you cease to be a child is when your parents are dead, so how, in my mother's opinion, can I possibly be middle-aged?

My menopause brings back memories of when I started menstruating (and it's interesting how many contributors to this book take as their starting point their first bleeding; and end with their last) which must have been when I was about thirteen. I had been anticipating it for some time, longing for it, almost. I felt I would be grown-up, at last, that my life would change in an instant.

My mother put me to bed with a hot water bottle and told me to rest until I felt better. I didn't feel ill; I had the smallest of stomach-aches, but I was awed by the sense of occasion and a little frightened by the bleeding, and so I lay there for most of the afternoon, willing myself to pass, ugly duckling-like, through this passage into a new, more exciting, world. Which I didn't. A bit of a let-down, really.

My periods ended abruptly. A hysterectomy at the age of forty-nine, while I was still menstruating, made me feel that I had been cheated of a 'real' menopause. From one minute to the next, a knife cut out my femininity, my identity as a woman, or so it seemed to me in my more melodramatic moments. That same knife also cut away my chance to have babies (babies I'd never really wanted, in truth). I wept about this loss afterwards, and sometimes still feel a sense of grief.

For the menopause does bring with it a sense of regret, though I suspect more to women, who, like me, have never had children. I've come to realise it's a good thing to acknowledge these feelings, and by doing so come to terms with them, to 'let go' of that childbearing stage of my life, and all that that entails, and move on to the next.

If I'm honest, I have to admit I still have a lingering sense of doors closing, a slight sense of lost opportunities and what-might-have-been. That last chance to have a baby has gone; there is the realization that there will be no continuation of my genes. On the other hand, my friends who have had children don't suffer from the empty nest syndrome, and in fact most have eagerly embraced the moment when their fledglings have flown. Much of their lives has been devoted to providing emotional, domestic and financial support to others, and now they have the chance to develop something just for themselves.

Certain events in my life, when viewed in hindsight, seem to me to be connected to my passage through the menopause. In my late thirties, I tried, laboriously and traumatically, to have a baby, but failed. My marriage ended in my early forties. When I was forty-nine, fibroids forced me, reluctantly, to have a hysterectomy. My physical menopausal symptoms were promptly treated with hormone therapy when they came, rather rapidly, as a result of the loss of my womb and one ovary. At fifty, I was made redundant from my job of twenty-seven years.

What a catalogue of woes! Actually, no; just life. Now I've ridden out the storm, I'm beginning to feel a sense of calm and a certainty about what I want. The depressions and mood-swings of those pre-menopausal years, my anxiety about the meaning of my life, have disappeared. The moment becomes important, and the pleasure in living too.

What I've now discovered, albeit tentatively, is a sense of widening horizons for myself; of the time to experiment and make discoveries; of the benefits of experience; and above all of a certain wisdom I've learnt through years of living to help me in exploring new avenues and possibilities. I like to think that my timidity threshold has been raised a few inches; that I can branch out, can say yes (or, perhaps even more importantly, no) to opportunities, that I can still achieve something worthwhile. And I get a certain satisfaction from the fact that, dammit, I've got this far.

I'm aware of the re-emergence of a sense of fun (last seen when I was a child, I sometimes think), a chance to relax now that all that striving of youth has passed, and I'm nurturing my silly side. I hope to acquire that rich belly laugh of middle age; I'm rediscovering the pleasure in friendship; the knowledge that pain does pass, eventually, and it's always possible, anyway, to laugh at myself.

It's interesting how much attention is being given to

books on the menopause by women at the forefront of the women's movement, such as Germaine Greer's invigorating and infuriating *The Change*. I find it encouraging that a subject that was until quite recently almost taboo – other than as a topic for the health pages of women's magazines – is now openly and vociferously discussed. The menopause has not only come of age, it's come out of the closet.

The hormone replacement therapy debate continues. It seems to me that health isn't really the issue. I assume – perhaps naively – that my doctor wouldn't prescribe something that will do me long-term harm, and I'm convinced by her arguments regarding the ability of oestrogen to protect me against osteoporosis and heart disease. No, what I feel the anti-HRT lobby is saying to me is: 'So you want to stay young, do you? Not prepared to admit to your age, eh? Trying to compete with those luscious younger women out there? Love your wrinkles, woman, why don't you? Acknowledge your crone status and shut up!'

My mother, like me, had a hysterectomy before she reached menopause (but, as she often tells me, she was fifty-five at the time, unlike my forty-nine years, and *she was still menstruating* – oh the one-upwomanship of bleeding!). But what this meant was that there was no maternal menopausal folklore to pass on, and it makes me realise how very important it is to have touchstones in these rites of passage; to have shared rituals, experiences, narratives, and myths.

In *A Certain Age*, the contributors seek to do just that – to present their imaginative interpretations of the menopause. All the writers have reached a stage in life where they have thought carefully about the subject, a stage when the menopause means something to them whether or not they have yet had it. They are strong and honest women, with rich interior lives, and their perspectives on The Change are not only interesting, they're positive and creative as well. Best of all, they're prepared to share their feelings.

For I've encountered resistance, elsewhere, to the idea of writing personally about the menopause. Refusals from potential contributors I've approached ranged from, 'Oh, I had no trouble at all. It affected me so little I don't have anything to say about it,' through, 'I really don't have time/ I haven't *had* it yet [outraged to be asked],' to, 'I don't want to admit to it.'

Admit to it? Well, there's a thing. Because what does admitting to – or anticipating – the menopause entail? It is, of course, all to do with our fear of ageing, the anxiety that the menopause may result in a loss of sexual attractiveness, and a lessening of the power, sexual or otherwise, that drives human beings, whatever their gender; an admission of the marks of the passing years, and, taking the anxiety to its logical conclusion, of starting on that long slide towards old age and death.

For me, admitting my fears to others, finding that they share some of them, helps me beat the bogies. I have been encouraged, stimulated and inspired by the contributions to *A Certain Age*. By their generosity and rage, humour and bad temper, good sense and care-lessness, vulnerability and strength, confidence and uncertainty, wisdom and frivolity, sexuality and modesty. In sharing their innermost feelings, these authors will undoubtedly bring a greater spirit of enquiry and openness, and a lessening of fear, to one of the great staging posts of every woman's life.

Peter Ruppert

CHANGES
Janet Burroway

HAIR

I was maybe thirty-five, six. I lay in a high bed between enamelled walls for one of those operations that needn't be named because it's unspellable. The black nurse arrived with basin, towel, soap, razor and ready cheer. I moaned, and the muscles of my stomach clenched, maybe with fear, maybe with more minor dreads, remembering the shaving of my pubes when my first son was born, my angry suspicion that it was unnecessary – and the long scratchiness of the hair growing out.

Now the buoyant nurse told me to turn on my side and raise a knee. Oh, I said, relieved, she wasn't going to shave me, then?

'Just in back! Oh, lord, love, I'm not going to take your glory!'

She drew the vowel out, voluptuous. I sighed with relief

and pride. My glooory. It was so. The hair on my head is fine and straight, the stuff I shave under arms, on shins, is negligible and spiky. But there! Then! A nether Afro, black with red highlights, luxuriant, an ebullient mass. Brushed, it would spring back instantly into ringlets. The American euphemism 'beaver' is ignorant, a thick flat metaphor, nothing like. But a 'bush', yes, resilient, silky, and sunny; it was a ready growth, warm May sprout, moss and glossy.

I remember the delicate baldness of girlhood, and how as a child I a little fearfully imagined myself in that goatee. Now, the other side of glory, I look at the thinness of my fur and find it somewhat stingy of nature, mean-natured, not necessary that I have become thus sparse.

Nobody, I take it, minds but me. It is not a death, a serious separation, is not a grief. I seem to function better, come to that, than in the glory days. Hormones are keeping my bone marrow dense, knowing better how to choose a lover keeps me at better joy.

More. I'm lucky. By the time she was my age my grandmother wore on her head a half-wig called a 'transformation'; by this age my mother's skull showed blue-white beneath the 'poodle' cut crimped to hide it; in his forties my brother was egg-pated above his beard. I've escaped this Pierce-side-of-the-family tendency to baldness, and my barber, who styles himself a stylist, tells me that there's no sign I'm thinning on top.

Only below, this bush of best youth, this kinky growth, this sable V, this little lawn, this springing grass, this private isle, reminds me that the very hairs are numbered.

What do you say to the losses of age? Oh, well. Oh, well.

TONE

K, who has a younger lover, moans that he's always wanting her on top. Why does she dislike this? I thought we fought through the fifties, the sixties, to gain the right to that position. I thought we wanted access to men who allowed, liked, preferred, requested it. I thought it was a distinct advantage of the younger lover, the liberated generation. I thought we fought to overturn 'missionary' laws.

No. I know perfectly well what she means. She says, 'Your face is so much better on your back.'

This is not very articulate, but it brings that discovery back with a rush. I was doing something sweet. P had no bedroom mirror, and I had a spare. This one was big and clear and old, with a many-times white-painted frame of heavy Victorian gingerbread. The glass was loose in the frame and I was going to secure it before taking it to him for long-term loan – an indefinite, commitment sort of loan. I drove the little nails around the back of the frame, covered the join with heavy tape, then turned it over on the carpet to check the paint for nicks. Straddled hands and knees over the silvered glass, I caught sight of my face. Stopped shocked. I watched the crawling creature warily. Its skin and chin pulled forward off the bone, the jowls slid into the hollow of its cheeks. The bold eyes hid under the shelf of brow, which furrowed with the grainy pucker of the pull of centre earth. The quality of the skin was that it foreshadowed its disintegration into cells of infinitesimal size. The opposite of taut is not, apparently, loose, but netlike. The wrinkles I am accustomed to seeing in my face are few and deep – laugh lines, crow's feet, furrows. These were hairline fissures dividing cell and cell.

This was not me. I know my bad side from my good, I know I am capable of posturing for the mirror, I know what I look like without make-up, I have even imagined my own skull. But this was not me, not me. I hung over gravity, I regarded myself gravely: I became grave.

Crepe is death's fabric.

All epidermis aspires to the condition of elbow.

Ageing is nature's own *Verfremdungseffekt*.

Because the idea of 'tone' is a metaphor from music, I have co-opted the word 'semiquaver' to describe this quality of skin. Dutifully doing the morning exercises that keep my spine from hurting, legs straight over my torso I watch my knees fall towards me, microcosms of erosion, miniatures of buckling earth, tan temblors of the meaning of change. The flesh semiquavers on my knees. I have become rather fond of the sight.

I ran into a very young woman at the vet's. In other times I'd have called her a girl. Her legs were thin and without definition, but with adequate fullness of lovely flesh. Her ankles ran straight from her calves into her sox and sneakers. Her skin was flawless Florida tan, butterscotch-pudding smooth. I admired this skin for several seconds before I realized that I did not envy and did not *want* it. I would call its texture callow. A lovely accident of flesh, and, lo, I'll choose my own.

You think I'm lying for rhetoric's sake, but don't underestimate the part of change that happens behind the skin. The beauty of bark, or woodgrain; the sound of 'texture': text-sure. I finger my lover's elbows forgivingly. We embrace in the frame of gingerbread. I like his ageing. I believe, know, that he likes my flesh buckling, semiquavering, text-sure. I like us liking our ageing. We feel, to me, to have traded some quality of mere appearance for superior sight.

I climb on top.

HILL

Aunt JJ, eighty-two, is touring Alaska once again with W, her companion of forty years. W is the elder, but will not say by how much. I keep their itinerary on my calendar because by the time I get back from England they will be packing for Switzerland, and we'll need to catch up. After

Switzerland it's the Delta Gamma convention, and then the World Future Conference. They live, when they're at home, in the Ozarks of Branson, MO, and JJ has lately taken to Country and Western. W keeps up a correspondence with some hundred and twenty people they've run into on their travels. Mornings they power walk, though they just call it walking. 'It's lucky,' W says, 'once you have the time, to have the health, the means, and the inclination still to travel.'

Meanwhile I talk to my stepmother, G, also eighty-two, in the nursing home in Arizona. First I call the nurse, who wheels G to her own phone; then I call her phone, which the nurse puts in her hand. G can walk, but won't; so the circulation has dwindled, and her legs are purple-blue. Amputation has been mentioned, though not to her. As soon as she hears my voice, she begins to cry. 'I just don't know how to cope with these interviews any more,' she says.

'What interview is that, dear?'

'Oh, well, you know your dad is always being interviewed by these magazines, and you never know exactly how much you ought to tell them.'

My dad died in 1987. So far as I know he was never interviewed by a magazine. G straightens the sob out of her voice and sighs. 'It seems like I just can't figure it all out. I don't know how to keep everything together.'

She knows, and means, that her mind is going, almost gone – though she articulates very clearly what she wants. She wishes she could dig a long ditch and just lie down in it and not get up. She wishes an angel would come and lift her out of all this mess.

I ask stupidly if she got the book, the sweaters. Does she see the picture of me and P on her dresser? Does she remember that we came out to visit her a few weeks ago?

'Couldn't you come over just for a few minutes now?'

'I'm in Florida, though. It's two thousand miles.'

'Florida!' she says. 'Florida!' G is in tears again, talking of the angel, whom I see with snow-white wings against a backdrop of Alaskan glacier. 'All these people, it's not that they mistreat us' – she is sharp enough to give the staff its due. 'But I can't do everything they want, gadding about all over the place. I can't. I wish that angel would come and wrap its wings around me, and just hold me until all this is over.'

I share genes with Aunt JJ, not with stepmother G. Mentally I ticket myself for Switzerland, the World Future Conference, thirty years from now. Still, it was G who, coherent a very few years ago, said to me, 'Oh, your fifties are wonderful, wonderful! I never felt better in my life than I did in my fifties. After that it kinda goes downhill.'

Do I believe her? I fear I do. I fear. I do. *Over the hill –* what a curiously apt expression after all! The driving and striving slowed, the view superb, you hand off the Sisyphus rock to the person on your left and, if you're lucky enough to have the health, the means, and the inclination, you stroll down the other side of the alp, working with gravity, gravity working with you. But don't relax; your job now is to put on the brakes a little. Power walk. Don't sit in the wheelchair, the wheels will do what wheels are meant to do. The angel is not always there when you need her, and stepdaughters are notoriously off in Florida.

TALE

Everyone has this story, the tale of the Goblin Obgyn, so it will not be necessary to tell it again, right?

No. True stories are believed only with frequent telling. So here is mine, not so long ago and far away:

When I was forty-five my second marriage ended with the end of his fidelity. I had been happy in the marriage, he hadn't gone out looking for an affair, but it had happened, and my trust had not survived. I had already been through divorce once, and this time I handled it, on the whole, pretty well – understanding that it's harder work to leave than to be left, and that it's easier to end a good relationship than a bad one. All the same, after a month or so I began to bleed and didn't stop for three weeks.

I went to my GP, a gentle and personable intern in family practice. I wasn't willing to go back to Dr B, the ob-gyn I used to see, I explained, because he had wanted to perform a hysterectomy for no better reason than that, in his opinion, I already had children enough. When I'd told Dr B I was not willing to fool around with my psyche in that way, he'd assured me that the loss of a uterus wouldn't bother me. (*Esprit d'escalier*: Shall we cut your balls off, then?)

Now Dr GP asked what I was doing to get myself through the divorce. I was keeping busy in the evening, I said, by getting cast in a play. I was recarpeting, for renewal in the house. I was lunching with women friends and driving to the coast every other weekend to be with my younger son in his summer stock company. If I felt I was in trouble, I said, I'd go for counselling.

'People pay thousands of dollars', he cheered me by assuring me, 'to learn how to cope like that.' All the same, for medical caution, he'd like me to see a gynaecologist. There was a new one in town, young, he probably wouldn't give me any nonsense.

At the new Dr M's, the nurse administered a haemoglobin test and stashed me in the cubicle. Dr M came in all brisk-and-clipboard, and began to take a medical history. I told him ('me and my big mouth' is the self-deprecatory phrase that comes to mind; in fact I think after all these years I am remarkably trusting, and that this is a virtue, not a lack) why I had not gone back to Dr B.

'B's a good man,' he said. 'If he wanted to take your

womb out, I probably will too.' I blanched and held my tongue. When M got to the advent, in my medical history, of a second dilation and curettage, he said, 'Good lord, two D&Cs. I'm certainly going to take your womb out. I'm not going to start manipulating you with hormones now!'

'No,' I agreed, dry. 'But I don't think there's anything wrong with my womb. I think I'm under stress. I'm going through a divorce.'

'I know, you're depressed and anxious.'

'No,' I said, 'I'm not. I may be later, but at the moment I'm very active, a bit hyper. It's my usual coping pattern.'

'You're depressed and anxious,' he repeated, as the nurse came in with the test results. 'That's funny. Your blood is normal.'

'I'm sure it is,' I said. 'I think this is a normal reaction to stress, and it'll abate of its own accord.'

'I'm the doctor,' he actually said. 'I'm not interested in the total picture, just my specialty, and then we'll slot it *into* the total picture. It's very clear that what you've got here is dysfunctional bleeding, and you'll need a hysterectomy.'

Dysfunctional bleeding? Is that a diagnosis? I thought that's the symptom I came in with. Hysterectomy? We cut out my uterus to slot it into the total picture? Is that some form of medical collage? Dr M, having diagnosed and prescribed, now left me to undress for the pelvic.

I sat for a minute seething. I powerfully did not want to be touched by his immaculate hands. I had a stabbing awareness of the times in my life when I would not have been able to get mad. I thought: just now it's important for me to feel good about myself. I can't afford the luxury of decorum.

I excused myself to the nurse. 'He's made me angry, and I'm not going to have the examination. I'll tell him so myself.'

I did so, with surface calm and under-rage. The doctor

sat rigid in his dignity. I was minutely mollified that he didn't charge me for the blood test.

Two days later I had a call from my ally Dr GP. 'I got to thinking about you,' he said in his pleasant way, 'and I thought maybe we ought to set up an appointment with a psychiatrist just to be sure, because, after all, you must be pretty depressed and anxious.'

Bewildered, I let him make the appointment, and it was a half-hour later that I tumbled to it, how the boys' network works. This had been one of the few times in my life that I acted, clean and immediate, on anger. I wondered, then, about those two D&Cs – were they unnecessary too? – and about the thousands of wombs that were waved away, this way, from women caught more vulnerable than indignant. I wonder now, having learned that flooding is a sign of the climacteric, which stress my body was undergoing, and when the medical establishment will turn its attention to such matters.

Luckily, the following Tuesday (my bleeding having stopped by then), I was able to convince the psychiatrist that I was sane in spite of my unseemly attachment to my uterus.

STAIR

Beginning in my teens I used to dream of a house through whose storeys I descended carrying a baby in my arms. The staircases would lead to doors that opened into rooms that opened on to staircases *ad infinitum*. The baby was damaged in some way – club-footed or, more often, wearing the medieval-painting face of an old man. I loved this offspring dearly, and would wake sad at its imperfection.

In my late forties, I dreamed that I had left the baby in the house in Sussex. I went to retrieve it – her? – but the house was full of strangers, tourists somehow, browsing through bric-a-brac for sale on a flagstone terrace above the lawn. The baby was upstairs, but though I could see the stairs I couldn't get to them. Someone said the baby wouldn't know me, and I was abashed, having no evidence it was otherwise.

One reading offered of dreams in general is that both babies and houses are the self, and I can make sense of that. Young, I felt that I carried my deformed self through the labyrinth of myself; middle-aged, I went to the self I had left behind to find a portion of my self that no longer claimed me.

Another reading offered is that the dream of babies is a dream of ova, those that can come to fruit and those that remain a thwarted promise in the body. I can make sense of that, too: the fearful weight of motherhood and then the poignancy of its loss.

But now I am thinking of the stairs. Between the fear of damaged babies and the regret of no more babies lie thirty-five years of friendship with the woman with whom I have discussed such notions. J is not my only confidante, but she is the one with whom this particular form of friendship most applies: that we talk the ideas of emotion. We cere-brate about feeling. We are moved by concepts. We analyse impulse. We noeticize sentiment. We fabulate explanation.

And the point is, I never dreamed of friendship. Whatever animal-deep, blood-dark feelings rule my dreams, friend-ship happened gradually in ordinary light. When J and I met it was at a tedious faculty-wives' tea. We got together because of trivial judgement on the local restaurants. We spent the first year over Scrabble, embroidery, TV; and have lived in the same town for only one six-month patch since then. Often we were apart for years without a phone call or a note, then took the conversation up mid-sentence. We ran into each other in London and then it seemed worth the trouble to meet in Belgium, Sussex, Illinois. When I divorced I went where she was. When I went mad she talked me through. When I was happy I discovered that I was telling her the story of my joy. When she went with her family to India I joined them, and we travelled together through Uttar Pradesh. ('Oh,' we still say in praise of each other's clothes, 'it's utter pra–desh!') When we travelled through the climacteric it occurred to us that we'd better not let a year go by without meeting somewhere, and now we do – sometimes alone, sometimes with our men in tow, in rental cars and rural restaurants, all four of us willing to honour the longevity of our friendship.

It's my luck that J is a family therapist, with a certain amount of codified knowledge about the stuff I write. I offer her fiction's insights too. Years ago she showed me her 'stair graph' of intimate relationship. People approach each other in the form of two facing staircases. At first they're far apart on the topmost tread; each takes a tentative step forward, towards the other. Then each descends into herself/himself, and if it seems worth the risk, the effort, takes another step. As long as they keep going into themselves and coming forward, the relationship gets deeper and closer, and can do so till death, though the stairs will never meet. If either refuses either motion – to plumb the self or face the other – the symmetry is skewed and the relationship will strain or break.

We were talking at the time – it will surprise no one to learn – about male-female relationships, and in particular the skewed-asymmetrical-strained quality of my own. The stair graph is a kind of image I can keep in mind even when I am dealing with bifurcating chaos in the gut; and it signally helped me in the area for which she intended it.

Only lately it occurs to me that J and I, ourselves, have demonstrated her graph: apart and together, delving into our selves and bringing forward what we've found; and that – for all the ova come and gone in our reproductive lives – we've created something that our subconsciouses did not warn us would be the stuff of life. Mating and maternity are in the blood; I have carried babies downstairs and gone upstairs to fetch them both literally and figuratively all the years of my adulthood. But no one is more clearly family to me than J.

In India it happened that we arrived at Fateh pur Sikri on the Feast of Id. I have a snapshot of the two of us, J and I, backgrounded by the brilliantly silk-swathed stalls, Laurel and Hardy in build, bare-armed and sweating in 110 degrees of Indian July, grinning ourselves towards each other down the ancient steps, old girls in an invented kinship, one step forward, one step down.

HELL

I wake under a feather duvet in a red cover, slightly jet-lagged. My stomach is clenched in a sickness of fear, which slowly reveals itself to be attached to something silly – a phone call I have to make, a repair to be seen to. My back aches too, and will never again *not* protest against an overnight aeroplane seat, so that this connection of travel and pain is a permanent feature remaining to my life. The fear sits sick, and spreads. Something about London, the bombardment from every side of ambition and accomplishment, the failure of socialism, the homeless on the corner, the posturing of heads of state. My own inadequacy. In a while I will get up, have coffee, do my exercises, have a nice day. Not yet.

In my middle forties I went through a period of two years in which I would wake and rage. The fury was unpredictable in its target. There was always something to attach it to – an imagined slight, a real injustice, an irremediable wound from the past. I resigned myself to the condition as permanent, something I had to endure because it was a part of me, probably the fruits of having repressed my anger for so long. Then I stopped drinking alcohol, adopted HRT, and wasn't angry any more.

Now usually I wake with anticipation, admire the plaster rose on my London ceiling or the real banana tree beyond P's Florida sliding door, which seems to give off the scent of the coffee he will bring me in a minute. Early-morning moods are rare, and I no longer believe they will outlast the comics page, let alone the calendar. But on the infrequent occasions when the dark ambushes me it is not as anger, but as dread; it takes me by surprise and hits with force.

I have no way of knowing which changes in my body, pysche, spirit, for gain or loss, have to do with menopause, and which have to do with ageing, or both, or how much of each. Jet lag, diet, muscle spasm, hormones – I consult the possibilities blind: I recognize recurrent feelings but I can't really judge what comes from situation, what from chemistry. Why should the black mood represent imbalance anyway, instead of simple insight? How much honesty is there in despair? How much of a figment is my usual busy cheer? Here, dark before dawn, muffled in feathers, how much more truth may I touch than in a day of doing?

A statistical analysis on page four of yesterday's *Guardian* shows that pessimistic people have a more realistic view than optimists, both of probabilities and of their own control over events. Optimists, however, *take* better control, and therefore accomplish more. *Ergo*, self-deception is functional.

When I was in college in the late fifties, in New York, I bought (from a bargain rack, it must have been, because I was too poor for new hardback books) Katherine Ann Porter's memoir *The Days Before*. The only memories of it I now retain are the pencil-soft portrait on the cover and Porter's observation that we trust hate more than love. Love, we think, needs to be coaxed and nurtured, carefully maintained; whereas impulses of contempt have the force of permanent truth. 'I love you' is always subject to review. 'I hate you' comes from the core.

Mostly, I have taken her observation as admonition. Why should we grant hate such force? Why should we think love so fragile when there's so much evidence of its resilience?

But isn't the answer simply: entropy? Both *eros* and *agape* shatter like a cup knocked on the floor. In some far future when 'future' is reversed, the universe contracts, and the past is yet to come, then the cup will jump back on the table and repair itself, hate will need fertilizer pellets, and love will cover the world like kudzu. But I can't imagine such a future, let alone believe in it, and in the meantime affection is fragile, compassion delicate. We are clumsy, ravenous, and short of time.

The image of E looms as I last saw her, her fierce despair and her cantankerous kindness. We said goodbye on the sill of the Sussex house she was about to lose to taxes, and that was before her paralysis as a writer, before morphine addiction, ten years before she died at ninety-two. My own life may seem to have come round to peace and safety. All the same, the rule is: death.

Abruptly I am off on my death run, worried for my friends, the world. I think X's health precarious, and R lives a grey half-life. Y may certainly have AIDS. Z drinks too much, and Q consumes herself protecting him. How fragile and out of control we are. I would touch wood, but that's too solid. Touch paper, touch leaf, touch cobweb.

I'm surrounded with people (young, but of my own age too) who think that the race will muddle through; that sense will solve the population problem, technology will restore the rainforests and the ozone layer, good will cope with the economy. What evidence supports such hope? Liberal democracy has triumphed and sells itself like laundry soap. Ethnic autonomy turns out to be bloody nationalism. England (England!) is pissing away its universities. Money represents not production but rumours of more money. This is not a recession, says J. It is the end of the world as we've (gluttonously) known it.

Serbia! Sarajevo! We have not given a thought to little Bosnia-Herzegovina for seventy-eight years, except I understand that the Orient Express went through, and the rugs were a splendid bargain. Bosnian refugees now are being processed through the Austrian camps through which P and his family moved after the Second World War. The lice are still there. 'Ethnic cleansing' fights for front-page space with the incipient collapse of Michael Jackson's plastic face. What do we learn? Are we worth saving?

Dread floods me like a hot flush. I see this will be one of those days dogged by clumsiness and tender skin. I will be too large, mincing, magnet to objects at the level of my thighs. No, I'll be all right. I'll be better once I've had coffee, done my exercises, made that call.

Not yet.

HEAL

I have no memory of stepping wrong off a boulder in the Chiricahuas. I was looking at the canyon, the climb of trees on the other side, the rim of stones like crumbling columns too tight-packed to fall – and the next thing I knew I was ass to the ground, one hand around a wrench of pain in my left ankle and the other clamping a palm full of flesh to the right knee. I figured the ankle was the more serious but that only an X-ray would see how serious. The knee I took a look at, prising my hand off by centimetres.

Pretty bad. The width of my kneecap, a deep scalloped flap like an upside-down cloud shape, cloud-pale but seeping blood around the edges – and is that bone, that bit? I'm aware not only of hurt and pounding heart but of incipient and protracted nuisance. Poor P. He'll have to look after me. He won't mind, but I'll be tense with apology. Our poor vacation, we'll hobble through the rest. Poor me. This is going to take a long time.

Hand clamped to the knee, blood seeping, I don't realize how long I've been there until I hear P calling.

'Jesus, why didn't you yell?'

I'm embarrassed to tell him I was embarrassed to have hurt myself.

It's children who are supposed to be repositories of awe. I don't think so. I think that children accept the natural miracles, and are dazzled only once they have a rudimentary notion of how things work, by things that appear not to – magic, cartoons, fireworks, 'effects' that are some way 'special'. I know that when I was little and skinned my knee, I took it as no great gift that the wound would sting and bleed. I endured the knowledge that my mother would get the dirt out whether I screamed about it or was brave. I knew it would stanch, and scab, and itch, and knit itself, probably with a little scar.

At fifty-five I watch this process with exploding wonder. It happens at wizard speed. The ankle produces its egg swelling within a couple of hours. I can walk on it next day, well enough to perambulate the border into Mexico, to shop for trinkets including a handsome carved cane. It's clear after all no bone is broken, and over the weeks as the swelling recedes it leaves a ring of delicate blue posies around my heel, which gradually, like posies, fade. The cut is an angry ruck of skin, which sucks itself back to its bed so hard that bending the knee becomes my major problem. I find I am fighting not the hurt but the healing, stretching against the eagerness of my flesh to knit. The blood fists into a dark scab, goes drab, and begins to lift around the edges. The shallower cut at each side of the kneecap smooths and flattens. Within a month, back in Florida in tepid Gulf salt water, I lose the scab and emerge from the ocean whole, just a slight double raised pink bloom on my knee, which looks a little tender, though it isn't.

My question is: why, when – even after a half-century, and after its ability to reproduce itself is past – a body not particularly well looked after will demonstrate its enthusiasm for survival in such wise, will speed goods about the veins, pump blood and antibodies, set itself to coagulation, osmosis, cleansing and creation, will mend so thoroughly that mobility and convenience are restored that could not be had from half a ton of technology – why, I say, should I ever have bitterly blamed it for such trifles as I have blamed it for: for having too much flesh in this spot, too little muscle in that, for producing this wrinkle, that sag, that grey hair, or this texture? Dear body! My dear body! It has gone about its incessant business with very little thanks.

I wake from a dream of D. We were having tea in a pleasantly shabby Victorian room, books and papers jumbled everywhere. 'What are you going to do next?' I asked, and she said, 'Nothing.'

'Ah.' I was a little disconcerted.

'Yes,' she said. 'I worked so hard early on that I feel I was cheated of my youth. What would you do, if you were going to make up for a lost youth?'

She seemed to want my answer. 'I'd get a good masseur,' I said. 'I'd have a good hard workout, and then a really deep massage.'

'I never thought of that.' She paid me a look of keen attention.

'Yes, and then I'd dance. I'd read, of course, and so forth. But, definitely, I'd dance.'

Waking, I know that I've been blatantly giving me good advice in my sleep. I giggle, reach my fingers out in a balletic gesture, meaning to touch P's back, but my forearm tumbles off the edge of the single bed, into the void under the red duvet. Oh yes. Another week before I'm back in Florida.

Okay. A week of friends and work. My ceiling rose is very pretty. I wrap myself for comfort, and in the hazy sleep-light I remember another quilt, the blue chintz with the cotton satin border that my grandmother made when I was – six? It was kapok-filled, the stuffing held in place by yarn ties; I remember her plump fingers pulling tight the knots.

There is a photograph of me on that quilt, spread on the spiky brown grass in front of the house on Alvarado Street. I am on my stomach, arms stiff in front of me, pointed toe touching my forehead over my arched back. I am ringleted like Shirley Temple, wearing a blue ruffled satin dance dress with tiny straps.

I remember too the buying of that costume, a miracle out of a rummage sale, one sleepy dawn when there was still such a thing as a vacant lot in downtown Phoenix, and the Women's Society for Christian Service had filled it with church tables covered in white paper and old clothes. I wandered among the rows while my mother sorted castoffs that Black and Mexican women waited in the hot dark to buy, for small change that the church would send to Africa.

I remember discovering the satin slip of a ruffled dress, pulling it out of a jumble of plaid cotton and scratchy wools. I remember my fear that some other mother would buy it before I could convince my own; and the hot quarter Mom slipped into my palm, which I handed over to the church lady behind the table: for satin, for ruffles. For a snapshot of a pose on the chintz quilt.

There are also photographs of me in pastel taffeta for the Gene Bumph revue, with silver sparkles on the yoke and a tilted pancake hat held in place by tight elastic; in a variegated fall of silk chiffon – turquoise, azure, emerald – when I danced a piece of seaweed to Ruth St Denis's octopus; in patent leather tap shoes with glossy bows and silver heels; in a pink tutu; in a red satin bum-skimmer skirt with white band jacket, gold Lurex frogs.

How I wanted to dance! And how persistently my body announced itself unfit for such endeavour. Apologizing for the extravagance of my lessons, Mom would laugh, 'I've got to do something about her, she's so clumsy!' Nor did this register as a cruelty, for I also thought our mutual desire was hubris. I was the stage child of a stage mother. I sat in the dark recital halls and made Shirley Temple *moues*.

At home my brother grunted while I practised acrobatics on the living-room rug. Chest rolls, backbends. 'Amos 'n' Andy' played on the radio; Dad sat at once inert and intent, because he loved a good 'show'. My mother darned. I did headstands with my head on a cushion and my hands positioned for a tripod; I did elbow stands with my soles against the door, while my brother sat on the couch mocking, saying: *Ugh! Ugh! I can do that too!*

There were toe shoes, little wads of lambswool, pain; and the satin ribbons crossed up my calves frenetically, as if I could will myself into a *prima*. There was a sheer rig in an autumnal theme, in the synthetics that had come in by then, skimpy on my solid pre-pubescent frame. There was the hateful, garish jester's costume when I became too thick for acrobatics and was cast as the physical equivalent of a straight man in what they dignified with the name 'Adagio'.

Wrong body, wrong body. I gave up the lessons, finally. I went to the North High basketball dances and stood in a corner in flocked nylon, praying for anybody to ask me on to the floor. I learned to jitterbug, defiant, and took a prize at it with my brother's college roommate. I learned to twist in time to chaperon my first college students. Once, in my thirties, I hired a teacher for a party, for a lark, during the disco phase.

My body, my poor body. When was it I learned to put on a tape and dance for me?

I stretch my ankle into a gingerly *point*, finger the polished scar. I think: dying, we heal. Over the hill, both body and psyche are still scrambling after order for themselves.

I know this. I learned very late why my love affairs ended in diminishment and recrimination. It's a long story that I can tell in a phrase or two: I always chose men I could not please. I worked very hard to understand this, and finally I understood it. I worked very hard to change, and eventually I changed. Bit by bit my psyche coagulated, scabbed and knit.

Now I bend my knee, caress its fresh bloom. The costumes turn in my mind, cutouts of photographs, afloat. They tumble around me in a slow free-fall. They are all there, the bows and the spangles, the chiffons wafting, the satin ruffles; they are putting me back to sleep. My duvet lifts and begins to lose its colour. It pales and floats as a cloud would float, unsupported in the middle air. Around me, Chagall-like, Aunt JJ and W go power walking on a nimbus. G's wheelchair spins, J is skipping down a stair, E is rocking back and forth over her Sussex sill. The world's a long way down.

I learned an interesting fact about detachment. Apparently the reason leaves fall is that as summer ends they suddenly produce a burst of fresh growth. They're so productive that the join at the matrix near the branch is weak. Then even a slight wind will break them off.

J said that older people find it necessary to detach, and do so in myriad ways. They get deaf, they don't remember. They relive their lives, go quiet, go inward, concentrating on self. Dying and healing in tandem, they go about the natural, necessary business of letting go.

This process is hardly begun in me. I have loving yet to

do. But I know what it means, I feel the beginning of it, on my cloud duvet. I have nearly learned that I can't control what happens in the world. I have nearly understood that I don't have to. I have nearly got it – that my friends and I are going to die, and that whether the planet offs itself will be decided without particular reference to me. I can do a little, and I'm responsible for the little I can do. I can give X a call tomorrow, recycle my trash, for instance. I can value P and celebrate my scar.

That's all. That's all I can do, and all I am required to do. In the grey half-light of sleep, I climb my duvet to dance.

George Frederick

PUBERTY MEETS THE MENOPAUSE
Kathleen Rowntree

She's got her arms in the sink, she's doing the Saturday wash – grey suds to the elbows, hair straggled out of its bun, specs smeared, nose dripping. I stare at her broad, stolid, unyielding form. Hate her.

Last Saturday she found a note in my skirt pocket, a daft bit of nonsense we twelve-year-old girls composed at school (to do with boys, naturally, and the way our as yet unapparent female charms will one day devastate them); she found it all soaked and crumpled from its dubbing in Persil, ironed it dry and smooth, deciphered it, *showed it to my father*. He was dragged forward to witness my denouncing. 'There, madam – explain this,' her eyes alight with that crazy look I've noticed in them lately, her body vibrating with anticipation. I don't really know what she's on about, what she's actually accusing me of, but I sense it's something outrageous and that she half hopes it's true, that she's taking unwholesome pleasure in her suspicions. Fearing my own disgust, I can't bring myself to establish what these suspicions are. I deny everything, stop up my ears, yell that she makes me sick. She won't find anything in my pockets this week, I think, watching her with loathing.

When I'm out of my room she sneaks inside, hunts through my drawers, inspects my knickers. She's waiting for me to 'start'. I'm sick with dread over this 'starting'. The way she talks about it (not 'talks' exactly, I don't give her the chance; more shouts after me), 'starting' is going to bring me down in some way. 'You'll have to listen to me then, my girl,' she says, clamping her lips together with grim satisfaction.

Hating her so much, I get scary premonitions that I won't always be able to contain myself. The time will come (perhaps my mother will be rubbing the clothes in the steaming sink and gloating over how it's going to come to me one day) when my hate will boil right over: I'll snatch the carving knife out of the kitchen table drawer and ram it into her self-righteously quivering back. There'll be a trial – it'll be in the papers; the judge will put a black duster over his wig and pronounce sentence; I'll be taken from my cell, they'll put a rope round my neck and everyone safe and snug at home will listen on the wireless as Big Ben strikes . . . Which will be so *unfair*, I think, watching in my bedroom mirror as self-pity rolls down my face in tears. All her fault.

One day, my father says, 'Your mother's going through a trying time. We must be patient with her.'

I report this comment to my school friends. 'It's the change,' they cry. 'Your mother's having the change.' And they back up this assertion with tales of bizarre behaviour on the part of aunties and grandmas, tales which have usually been confided by their mothers. These girls are lucky. It's all right for them. Their mothers are youngish with jolly lipsticked mouths and pretty hair; you could talk about anything with these mothers without ever feeling sick or threatened. My own mother is oldish and untidy-looking, big and downright, a good woman, a manager. She's the headmistress of our village school, she runs the Mothers' Union and a Bible class. Everyone respects and admires her. Village women of the sort who are always getting pregnant, or kept short of money by their husbands, or have delinquent children, depend on her. She dispenses advice on street corners, she organizes whip-rounds, she visits the squatter families in the old Nissen huts. She cycles everywhere – to school, to church, to meetings in town. On Saturdays, she does the weekly wash while my sister and I supposedly dust and hoover. (In fact we switch on the vacuum cleaner, then stand about reading her library books – she doesn't check, the noise satisfies her, and she's never been known to notice dust.)

No one could ever have called her pretty. But there were things about her I liked, such as the feel of her soft, slack cheek, the chink of the green glass beads on her one and only necklace as they swung from her neck, her nice grave eyes. These eyes, though, have gone dark and huge: mad-looking. Her skin is mottled and drab. Her untidiness has got worse: her petticoat invariably shows, her shoes are battered, the straps of her vests are held in place with safety pins, the necklace is broken and tossed away in a drawer.

It gives me quite a turn to discover the same insane look that dilates my mother's eyes in the eyes of the village postwoman. I'm taking a parcel from her at the time; I look up and catch her leering at me. Mrs Rose (the postwoman) has a reputation for unsavouriness due to her spending every evening in the pub and there being no Mr Rose despite the fact of her three daughters. So Mrs Rose is having 'the change' too, I think. Although at first it's stunning to discover a link between my esteemed mother and the raffish Mrs Rose, on further reflection it doesn't surprise me; after all, *I* know that my mother is estimable only on the surface; underneath she's disgusting, prurient. Of course, by now I have been informed that 'the change' is to do with female biology. Even so, it never occurs to me to associate myself with the phenomenon. (I'm only thirteen; I think I'm going to live and bloom for ever.) Nor do I have the slightest sympathy for my mother. My feeling about it is that if she's got this condition, she's to be condemned and despised. This must be so because of the vileness emanating from her.

And why should she vent this condition on me? Why do *I* incense her? So far as I know she doesn't accuse other people of nameless wrongs, find the very sight of any other person reason for outrage. Sometimes, without warning, she springs out on me, grabs me to her, thrusts her face so close to mine that as she rants and accuses me of things her breath gets into my nose and her spittle lands on my lips. I can't hear what it is she's accusing me of; all I catch is the rasp of her voice, her mad fever. Through her gripping fingers I feel the current charging her, gross, obscene.

This state of affairs continues for some years, during which I learn the proper name for her affliction: the menopause. (For the next two decades this word will make me uneasy, will conjure dark things without a name; things which all sane non-menopausal creatures will naturally shun and loathe. Read the word, hear it, and quick, before I smother it, comes my instinctive recoil – switch off the radio, turn the page, think about something else; the sort of response which once led to witch-burnings, I remind myself severely.)

When one of my more advanced school friends discovers tampons, I sit with a huddle of girls in the cloakroom listening as she describes their convenient use and benefits. We pore over the inscrutable diagrams. Our instructress tells us not to worry: if you make a few passes, the thing just slips in, sort of finds its own route. The great thing is, you just drop them down the bog afterwards, pull the chain on them. I suddenly see what tampons can do for me – provide sanctuary from my prying mother who is always searching for evidence of my time of the month, totting up days and sending me speculative glances. I'll no longer have to find new hiding places and stash malodorous parcels in my satchel to take to school for disposal (away from her greedy sight). My friend takes me to Boots to help me make my first purchase. It's like freedom dawning.

I start looking my mother in the eye; feel smugly, confidently, that I've outwitted her. One day I interrupt her ransacking my chest of drawers. My things are tossed everywhere; a lack of the evidence she requires has brought her to the boil. She lunges at me, accuses me of doing things with boys, screams that she knows I'm in trouble and the shame and disgrace will kill my father and how Mrs Robinson, her arch-enemy on the school management committee, will crow, and really I'm no better than that Mary Tanner down Ing's Lane. She means pregnant, I think incredulously, backing into the wall, yelling for my father's protection. He comes puffing up the stairs and into the room; pulls her off. He can tell from my childishly frightened face that she's got it all wrong, that this time she's gone too far.

By the time I'm sixteen, my mother is calming down. Now she starts collecting fractures: hits a rut in the road when she's cycling to church, falls off, breaks her arm; smashes her shoulder when the table she's standing on at school collapses as she's reaching up to hang the Christmas decorations; skids on slimy autumn leaves, falls awkwardly, fracturing hip and femur. She endures increasing pain from these fractures stoically, seldom complains, but always has a pile of codeine tablets by the side of her plate at mealtimes to take with her coffee like after-dinner mints. When high-strength codeine is made no longer available without a prescription, she gets terribly anxious; aspirin's useless, she says, and she hasn't got time to kick her heels in a doctor's surgery.

I get married. We have wedding group photographs taken. When these arrive, I know there's something odd about them; it takes me a while to work out what this is. Then it hits me: my mother has shrunk. She used to be an imposing woman, stood at least two inches taller than my father. Now, he dwarfs her. Also, she's become distinctly humpbacked.

I'm expecting my first child. I'm standing at the ironing board in our flat one morning when the baby quickens and an outsize fear grabs me. What if it's a girl? A girl who will one day regard me as I once did my mother, who will look at me and sweat with loathing, feel disgust rise in her like bile and horror beat in her chest like a trapped bird. I set down the iron. For the first time in my life, I realize, I've associated myself with the menopause. It may happen to me. (All right, *will* happen.) But my kids will be past adolescence by the time it does, I frantically calculate, will probably have left home, so won't be around to witness my degeneration. And with luck they'll be boys rather than sharp-eyed, knowing, condemning girls. Oh, God . . . Although I've long since abandoned religion, no longer believe in God, no longer pray, I start praying now. Dear God, I beg you, I implore – let this baby be a boy.

In time I have two sons, no daughters. My shrinking, increasingly humpbacked, multifractured mother and I become firm friends. We see films and plays together, go on shopping trips, laugh, argue, run up shocking phone bills. Her company is a pleasure; she's one of the most enlivening people I know. But one topic we never touch on is female biology. If the subject arises accidentally when we're both within earshot, I leave the room or change the subject.

For her seventieth birthday I take her to Florence. She's never flown before, she's like an excited child, entranced by everything from a bird's-eye view of the Alps to the cunningly designed in-flight meal in its plastic compartments and cellophane sachets. With her stick and guide book, she veers round Florence on uncertain legs, marvelling at a new and wonderful world. One evening, coming down in the lift, a chap I've seen working on the desk in the hotel asks me out to dinner. I'm thoroughly taken aback, stammer thanks but that of course I'll be eating with my holiday companion. 'Oh no, dear, you go; no need to stay in with me, go and enjoy yourself,' she urges, lewd mischief lighting her eyes, which dart from his face to mine. I seize her arm, drag her from the lift, confront her. She's all blank unselfishness. I shove her into a chair, go and fetch our pre-dinner drinks. It's her old menopausal demon raising its head, I think, reluctant to return to her. Then, during dinner, I dismiss this idea. She's so animated – enthusing to the couple at the next table about the Spanish Chapel in Santa Maria Novella, getting into a pickle with her *linguini pesto*, exclaiming over the *Zuppa Inglese*: she hasn't an idea what the consequences of accepting such an invitation might be, I tell myself; she's a veritable innocent abroad.

But that night, I'm self-conscious about sharing a room with her; feel prickly using our bathroom; lie awake listening to the click she makes in her throat. I know I'll never manage to blot out how she was all those years ago, or smother the memory of the hatred I once felt. I think of this hatred as a set-aside familiar artefact, like her old green glass necklace, once worn daily, now stuffed to the back of a drawer: I don't need to take it out to remember how it feels, how it looks. And I know *why* I hated her. It was because she was going through the menopause – going through it, all right, nerves screaming, mind skewed, bones crumbling, for years. I can manage pity for her now, alongside my revulsion. Also fear for myself.

The fear dissipates. I'm in my confident forties, the children grown, possibilities opening up for me. 'Menopause' becomes a word I can live with. This is due in large measure to several of my friends sailing through it unscathed, in some cases barely noticing the phenomenon. A feeling develops that this is the modern way, that suffering and verging on craziness belong to the bad old days. I begin to take a mild interest in the subject, cut out articles in newspapers that may come in useful later on for the addresses they give, the books they mention and their sensible-sounding courses of action. I store these cuttings in my bedside drawer. (But do I really believe I'll ever get to the stage when I need to consult them? Deep down, is facing the menopause any more conceivable than facing death?) Putting these clippings away in the drawer gives me a feeling of having dealt with an unlikely occurrence. Reading them before I store them away convinces me that the menopause has been taken in hand.

It's a good time for me now; I've never felt nor looked better. Nevertheless, I catch myself speculating on my physical inheritance. It's most unlikely that I take after my mother, I decide, for my mother was once a large woman, whereas I have always been small; much more probable that I will go the way of the grandmother I resemble. I make discreet inquiries as to the health and disposition of this lady in the later half of her life. No mention of bizarre behaviour or swings of mood or bone fractures, thank goodness. Not that I waste much time on these reflections – mostly I'm thinking of other things altogether. When a doctor adds the proviso 'at your age' to what he is telling me, I smile smugly, sense my inner equipment turning like a Rolls-Royce engine with plenty more miles on the clock.

Then – calamity. I'm fifty; my doctor discovers a large and rapidly expanding internal growth. I require a hyster-ectomy. The surgeon airily proposes also to remove my ovaries: one has already been submerged by the growth; the other is bound to give up the ghost as a result of the op. At your age, she adds.

Not *my* ovary, I retort, jolly well leave it alone.

A few weeks after the operation I have a blood test to measure my hormone level. It will be a fortnight before the results are known. I feel tired, a bit weepy, but of course this is all down to the anaesthetic.

My menopause lasts approximately six hours. Very short, very frightening. One morning, I'm crossing the yard when it strikes me how desolate the garden looks, how heartbreaking the sight of green buds shooting, how vain and pointless the effort involved in sap rising. I break down, can barely get back into the house for sobbing. Then a wave of fire shoots through me, makes my hair stand on end. I sit down, remember about 'hot flushes'. Decide the phenomenon can be no such thing; I must be running a sudden fever. But desolation overwhelms me; I lie down on the floor, feel the cold flags beneath the thin carpet, think about tombstones as my heart races. Eventually, on the windowsill above my head, the phone starts ringing. It's the surgeon's secretary. She tells me to go at once to see my general practitioner who has been instructed to start me on hormone replacement therapy. My oestrogen level has gone from high to virtually nil. Haven't I noticed any symptoms? she wonders.

It's breathtaking how swiftly the little transparent patch I stick on my bum dispenses well-being throughout my system. Six weeks later I'm on a hill-walking holiday in north-west Majorca. I'm so lucky, I think guiltily, next time I face my mother. She's looking at me curiously, her eyes full of unasked questions. You were born too early, I silently tell her; I'm going to escape what happened to you.

Within a year, shrunken, spine so bent and crooked it makes my heart jump when I rearrange her pillows and inadvertently touch it, old fractures so numerous they can't decide from the X-rays whether her latest fall has resulted in a brand new break, my stoical, lively-minded mother dies, just three days short of her ninetieth birthday. On her death certificate is written *osteoporosis*.

Mother, I loathed you once. You made my flesh creep. I wanted to smash you, wipe you out. Never felt that about anyone else – nor about you, since. It was your menopause.

MY MENOPAUSE
Molly Parkin

I began bleeding at eleven. I was the first in my form at school, alongside a vivid Jewess called Rosalie. We looked like sisters, people said, but I couldn't see it myself. I would stare at her in class trying to fathom where the likeness lay – she with her cloud of thick, black hair, her green eyes, the mysterious shapeliness of her small body.

I acknowledged that we resembled each other more than the rest of the girls in this English school. The fact that I was Welsh and she was Jewish set us physically apart from our fair, leggy, flat-chested counterparts. But I wanted to be what I had always been – a naughty tomboy, a rough-and-tumble girl, good at games and getting my clothes torn and my knees scraped, not a dainty *femme fatale* like Rosalie Dancyger.

The bleeding changed everything.

It started in bed, an hour after our cat gave birth to four kittens beneath my blankets. My mother was furious, having to change my laundry twice in one night. She scolded me in the bathroom, whilst I was still shivering from the double shock of the kittens' blooded bodies stuck to my nightie, and the sensation of my own blood oozing from that same place that had produced the kittens from the cat. In my confusion I must have made a connection between the facts, expecting that any moment I too would give birth to my own furry offspring. In the meantime all I could do was tremble at the scarlet dribble staining the cold lino, woefully aware of my mother's displeasure, watching as she made a makeshift sanitary belt from garter elastic, to which she pinned a length of torn-up sheet.

'Wear this between your legs until the bleeding stops,' she said. 'It'll take about a week, maybe longer.' She passed me the old sheet to tear up into more clumsy nappies.

'A week!' I yelped. 'But what about school, and games, and riding my bike?'

'What about it?'

I looked down at the thick fold of cotton poking out the front and the back of me. It felt as big as a bolster. How could I walk with this between my legs? I ventured a few steps. Blood spurted out of the side. I started crying. 'This is HORRIBLE!'

My mother sighed, nodding. 'A woman's lot. We all have to bear it. Two things to remember: not to catch cold, and not to have a bath. And most important,' her voice dropped to a harsh whisper, 'don't ever let your father know when you're "on". It's a private thing. It's not nice for other people to know, especially not men.'

'How long am I going to have to put up with all this?' I snivelled.

'All the way through to middle age. Right through to The Change. The truly worst time', she added darkly, 'in a woman's life.'

★

My mother's bleak view had always, certainly, been coloured by her own emotional difficulties and that unlivable-with darkness in her, which I don't doubt contributed to the premature death of my father. At the very time that she proffered this dismal glimpse of my physiological future, she was suffering the effects of a recent hysterectomy. So she herself no longer bled.

Over subsequent years – years interspersed with her increasing recourse to psychiatric wards following yet another unsuccessful attempt at suicide – she would solemnly ask if I was 'still bleeding'. It was as if she imagined that I had never stopped from the age of eleven. That the first period was still flowing. Even on her very death-bed, when I was fifty-three and she was eighty-one, she pleaded the same question and received the same grim affirmative.

'Pray God, it will be over soon.' She lifted her eyes to heaven. 'Then watch out.'

Days later she was dead. I still cannot be certain to what she was referring – my oncoming climacteric or her departure from this earth. I believe the thought of the former dismayed her far more than the other. This was my mother, my role-model.

I am sixty now, and have not bled for five years. The stormy passage my mother prophesied for me most certainly came to pass. At the time I was in such chronic confusion and pain for other reasons – not least the loss of her – that I never connected 'my change' to these matters. But now, in hindsight and from the view of current calm harbours, I see that my mother was probably right. The chaos of those years was largely self-inflicted, the events merely the mill-stones of menopause, my catastrophic response being not too unusual given my time of life.

★

A particular foretaste of gloom entered my soul at the loss of the child I was expecting with my second husband. I was thirty-nine, and we had both wanted this baby very much. It would be the infantile link with each other that our dearly beloved existing children, from other marriages, could not supply.

I had just been made fashion editor of the *Sunday Times* and, pleased though I was at the promotion, the baby meant much, much more. When I miscarried in the fourth month I chose to see it as a punishment from Above, for the abortion I'd undergone at the time of my first divorce. I hadn't wanted that abortion, but I had been warned that I might well lose custody of both young daughters if I appeared pregnant in the dock. That's just how it was in those days.

A week after my miscarriage a decade later I took part in a television programme on abortion, certainly a moral hot potato then. My mother was so appalled that I should admit to it in public that she refused to speak to me for months because of what the neighbours would have thought. The programme was hosted by Malcolm Muggeridge, who afterwards wrote me a kind letter saying that he felt that I had been severely damaged by experiences in my life and felt that he could be of help. I used the letter to entertain cocktail party guests, holding the offer up for ridicule. But something about it actually did touch a profound core of sadness in me which I certainly refused to acknowledge. I had never allowed myself properly to grieve either the child of that miscarriage or the child of the abortion – not until now. Now, when, at sixty, I inquire into my past, learning as I do so to forgive myself and cherish the girl and young woman I was, as much as I nurture the person I have become today. The only way I knew of coping then with any disturbing emotion was to drink, to drink until I was paralytically drunk . . .

*

I didn't start drinking at eleven, though if I had known that it would have enabled me to accommodate the avalanche of male attention that came my way when I started bleeding, I certainly would have. Rosalie Dancyger and I were the only girls wearing brassieres, the only ones who so clearly needed them.

The effect of these breasts, these appendages, these monstrous mammary glands, was appalling to me. However I dieted, whatever ludicrously low weight I managed to achieve, I could never lose my pert pals. They were with me for life, attracting lewd comments, wolf-whistles, stray fingers, stolen caresses, Tom, Dick and Harry. They made summer a nightmare, running for buses impossible, cleavage unavoidable. They took over my blouses, my sweaters, my T-shirts. They took up residency when I started bleeding, occupying the space between my chin and my waist with a boldness that belied everything I had ever felt about my body.

I blamed the blood and the breasts for all the bother I got into with boys. If they hadn't started I would have been all right. I'd had a varied romantic career, to say the least, by the time I stopped bleeding. I'd been through two divorces and nine fiancés. My first marriage had lasted for seven years, my second for eleven. I was forty-eight when this marriage finished. Now would start the period of my greatest promiscuity.

Sex, sex with strangers, became as much of an addiction as those two which already held me in vicious thrall – alcohol and nicotine. I had dabbled with drugs, such as cocaine, in New York – a year spent in Hades at the very end with my second husband. But now sex gave me the same charge as a line of coke. I chose to refer to it as my form of literary research. I boasted that my role of sexual predator gave me material for the comic-erotic books which I was still managing, just about, to crank out. But the chronic need to lure men – the firmer the flesh, the larger the penis, the better – actually sprang from a craving more desperate than that. Having been used, all my menstruating life, to male attention on a lavish scale, I had now decided to play the game with my own set of rules. I used men as I feared they may have used – abused – me. I was getting my own back at last.

I caused a considerable number of human beings a great deal of pain in these years: almost a decade lasting from my late forties through to my fifty-fifth birthday. I crucified relationships between couples, long or short, left, right and centre. If Rosalie Dancyger had ever been a *femme fatale* on a juvenile scale, then I was the gruesome adult version. No man, it was said of me, was safe in my presence. I simply had to have them all, whether they appealed to me in a sensual, intellectual, spiritual sense or not.

This was madness, insanity. In earlier years, pre-feminism, it would have been described in clinical or social terms as raging nymphomania. But that word, with its critical connotations, had fallen out of favour. Now I was heralded as a truly free spirit, in tune with the sexual times, the liberation of women, the vanguard of sexual equality.

I was interviewed ceaselessly on my views about aspects of this personal freedom – on one-night stands, for instance, and on men as sex objects. My statements were coarse and controversial enough to ensure maximum publicity and yet further coverage. But much as I appeared to glory in this, a part of me flinched, shrank away from the strident persona. My inner voice spoke softly. I didn't like what it said. I drank to drown the sensitive side which was struggling against becoming totally submerged. I began to identify more and more with my mad mother.

Having lived a year of total depravity, sex orgies, drink and drugs for the final year of my marriage, at the infamous

Chelsea Hotel in New York, I moved to Wales to be with my now-senile mother until her death.

Understanding that when she went my world would finally crumble, despite the continuing love of my daughters and the rest of my close family and loyal friends, I went up to the top of the mountain and asked for help. I had been the financial and emotional rock for many people for many years, yet now, in my vulnerability, I felt I had nowhere to turn. There was nobody to whom I felt I could break down and cry. My mother was out of reach – alive, yet no longer there. My overwhelming pride would not permit me to ask for help from any other source. And besides, what would I be asking for, help over what exactly? Alcoholism, which I still had not acknowledged within myself, is a disease of denial. It insists that you don't have it until you reach your utter rock-bottom, physical, emotional and spiritual. Appallingly, I was yet to sink even further than I had sunk so far.

Until that journey to the top of the mountain, I had not acknowledged the God of my childhood for many decades. The path I had chosen in adult years was worlds away from the Welsh chapel which had meant so much in childhood. I put out my hands and beseeched God either to take my life or to show me how to live it in some kind of grace and dignity. These two words had meant very little to me until now. But the force of self-preservation had intimated that I could simply no longer continue unless something changed. What I was actually yearning for was peace of mind.

That was the turning point. In hindsight, I see that what altered was my attitude. I had surrendered, and help was at hand.

It is difficult for others to understand, when I deny that it was my strong willpower that enabled me to come to terms and eventually overcome my three addictions. Difficult to grasp that the recognition of my difficulties is what led to recovery. My emergence from the living hell had little to do with strong willpower, everything to do with facing up to myself and admitting the powerlessness.

If I had continued on that path, I would certainly be dead by now. The mystery – though it is no mystery really, just as there is no such thing as coincidence – is that as my bleeding lessened, so did my drinking. When one ceased, so did the other.

I was fifty-five when, at 7.30 p.m. on 23 March 1987, I went to a self-help group for alcoholism. The date and the time will always be emblazoned in my brain. On my way out from the very first meeting I dumped the four packets of cigarettes from my handbag into the dustbin. I haven't smoked since, though my consumption was up to a hundred cigarettes a day.

My promiscuity – on an hourly, sometimes six-men-a-day, one time eleven-in-an-evening basis – disappeared altogether, to be replaced by a celibacy which lasted for the following four-and-a-half years. Last year I visited Greece with a group of close friends and dispensed with my celibacy *à la* Shirley Valentine. Actually, my Greek lover was the gorgeous outcome of a ritual I conducted with two pals at Athens Airport on our return journey. We dumped what we referred to as 'our bodily shame and sexual inhibitions' in the dustbin, and each asked for a lover. In truth I asked for three lovers: the first to be a Latin, larger than life and about my age; the second to be an intellectual companion to take me to the ballet and the opera; and the third to be a beauty with the smooth skin and chiselled lips of the Greek waiters who had served us all week.

The first – to the amazement of my companions, not to mention myself – came into my life within the hour. I met him on the plane and was enjoying five-star sex in the five-star hotel on the edge of Hyde Park that very evening.

The two other requests turned up in a matter of weeks. Whenever I ask the Universe for anything, it always transpires – but not always with such alacrity. Since this particular ritual was conducted in such a spirit of fun, it must have found particular favour. I acknowledge all my gifts, my small miracles, with gratitude. I understand now that God intends all his children to be happy, joyous and free.

All my God-given gifts have been returned in my sobriety, in what I see now as my glorious post-menopausal years. It had always been understood from earliest childhood that I would become either a painter or a writer. I had always excelled effortlessly in these subjects at school, but I had chosen art school instead of university, painting instead of writing, as my chosen profession.

When my periods began at eleven, and my life changed so dramatically, the art provided a refuge, an escape. My odd clothes as an art student were consciously eccentric enough to put conventional youths off. In fact the clothes have continued to do just that. It is my way of weeding out the less intrepid admirers, of at least honing things down to kindred spirits.

In my years of madness, of course, it made no difference to me what my male victims thought of me – my clothes, my body, my age. I was simply the predator, and they the unfortunate prey.

My Painting Muse, as I refer to her, walked away with my husband. I kicked him out on the Saturday, and on the Monday morning, when I went upstairs to my studio, she was no longer there. The devastating creative block remained with me for the next twenty-five years, such was the trauma of that first split. The fact that my drinking increased to such an extent that my inspirational channels were permanently clouded must have been one cause. But I managed my next careers perfectly well without calling a halt on the alcohol consumption – until those careers too, successful as they had all been, finally petered out.

When the painting ceased, at the high point of one canvas having been purchased by the Contemporary Art Society and housed in the bowels of the Tate Gallery, I moved effortlessly into the world of high fashion. This was the swinging sixties, when anyone could – and was encouraged to – do anything. I opened my own boutique, the second in London. Biba was the first, run by my friends Barbara Hulanicki and her husband Fitz. In a matter of weeks I was invited by a new glossy magazine, *Nova*, to become their fashion editor. Such was my success that I went on from there to become fashion editor of *Harper's Bazaar*, then I was headhunted by the *Sunday Times*. In 1972, the same year that I left the *Sunday Times* to start writing novels, I was presented with the Fashion Editor of the Year Award. I had spent a decade in the heady world of *haute couture*. Now I was to spend the next decade on the bestseller list, writing fiction. I wrote as prodigiously and prolifically as I had ever painted. The novels flew from my fingers, one every year. At the same time I published a book of poems, a collection of journalistic pieces in book form, and a recipe book for sandwiches.

The final three novels I wrote, each of them, in a fortnight. I wrote around the clock and each time almost sustained my first coronary. That's how incapable I was any longer of planning my work properly and fulfilling the publishing deadline without this last-minute desperation. I was simply losing control.

The wildness of my after-hours was starting to take over. I could no longer concentrate on producing even the simplest piece of journalism. I had been banned from 'Pebble Mill at One', and the word was going around that, good value though I might be on television, I could no longer be relied upon to turn up sober. The engagements started to dwindle, and eventually fell away altogether.

I embarked at the age of fifty-two on the only career left open to me. I could still make people laugh in the clubs and bars and parties, so it was suggested to me that I go in for it professionally and get paid at the same time. I wrote a one-woman show of risqué poems and anecdotes lifted from my own life. I got a theatrical agent and took to the stage.

The show was an immediate success. First I performed with John Cooper Clarke, the punk poet, on the stage of the Young Vic in a poetry festival. From there I was on at Ronnie Scott's, and I did the Edinburgh Festival two years on the trot. The final time was in the largest venue at the Assembly Rooms, with the largest poster – a sellout business. I toured nationally to the same response, but had my comeuppance in Dublin, in the Festival. I did my final show there in an alcoholic blackout. The audience walked out and demanded their money back. I have yet to meet another person on this earth, male or female, who has been banned from Dublin for drinking, as I was. I rate it as one of my rarer distinctions.

But this final humiliation led me towards recovery – that and the fact that my youngest daughter announced that she was starting a family. It had always been my greatest cause of despondency that my mother could never completely fulfil her role as a responsible grandmother. Now I could see that I would lose the company of my own grandchildren in the same way if I didn't stop drinking and pull my life into some kind of order.

It had always seemed to me wickedly unfair that a woman, as she is approaching the most difficult time of her life with the change, should suffer the loss of various – if not all – of her given roles up to that time. By this I mean that it is quite probable that one or either of her parents could die at this time, as my mother did. So I had lost the role of daughter.

My daughters were now living their own independent lives, so that my role of mother, as I had known it, was no longer there – certainly since I had become so utterly irresponsible and such a social liability to them in drink.

I was no longer a wife. Like many other wives of my age – or rather, ex-wives – I was meant to grin and bear it as I congratulated each of my ex-husbands on their marriages to younger women. Another role lost.

The brutal fact is that the change is what it says – that the life you honed for yourself in all these past years is no longer there, cannot be relied upon to continue. Age has caught up, and the future is a dark void. The time has come to start getting to know Self.

I am now at the glorious stage of having achieved what before was impossible. I have learned how to live in the day. All recovering alcoholics understand and live by this principle: that it is dangerous to project and claim that you will never drink again. All we say is that we won't drink, or will try not to, just for today. Since this has worked so magnificently for me regarding alcohol and cigarettes for the past five-and-a-half years, I now apply the same principle to other areas of my life.

I don't lose my temper any more. I vow not to do so, every morning, just for today. I don't cheat, or steal, or beg, or borrow – just for today. I have forsworn my greatest weakness: I don't gossip, gossip maliciously – just for today.

When events threaten to unhinge me, as they can but hardly ever do any more – compared to the way my life was once: a series of high-emotion explosions, with me as the drama queen of all time at the centre – I now quietly repeat the prayer that we use in our self-help groups: 'God grant me the serenity to accept the things I cannot change, the courage to change the things I can, and the wisdom to know the difference.'

That gives me strength, that gives me certainty. That shows me that I no longer need to struggle ever again on my own. The help is there whenever I reach out and ask for it.

My spirituality is the source for me. I have always understood that. Even in those long years in the wilderness, in the shadow of the valley of death, somewhere deep inside I understood that. When I respond to a sunset, to the core of another person, to the warmth that floods my soul when my grandchildren hug and kiss me, I know that this is what true spirituality means.

My flame, that spiritual flame, was barely flickering for so long that the journey to my present joy, where the light is strong and true, was also slow and long. It had to be. The gifts came inch by inch, but each one brought a further marvel in its wake.

My painting came first. I was returning from a women's self-help group and walking back through Hyde Park in the first summer of my recovery. It was evening and the sky was scarlet, silhouetting the same trees which I had painted so many times years ago as my babies slept in their pram beside me. The familiar pain of no longer being that same artist stirred inside me, but then a small voice bade me draw the scene on the back of an envelope, in pencil. I became so absorbed that before I'd realized it the sky was full of stars. It was dark and I was locked in the park. I had to climb over the railings at Kensington Church Street to get out.

The same inner voice told me to purchase a small sketchbook and some watercolour paints – me, who had always spurned such humble forms of self-expression before, used as I was to vast canvases and passionate oils. I started humbly from there, and within a month I found myself in the Arctic on a luxury liner painting and writing about the trip for the *Sunday Telegraph* magazine. Many travel assignments for various magazines and newspapers have followed since then: Egypt, Tahiti, the Caribbean, India. Another career – yet another – as travel writer, one who can illustrate her own articles, has fallen into my lap unexpectedly.

And I have become an Agony Aunt, a role close to my heart, one of the few jobs that I had not tried in Fleet Street by the time I left. I am the Agony Aunt for the mass-circulation *TV Quick* magazine. I love it! I get about a hundred letters a week, and publish the replies to about six in the magazine. That's all there's room for. But everyone has a reply if they include their address; my assistant helps me with that. Many of the letters come from middle-aged women suffering from the menopause, feeling that their lives are over, just as I did so relatively recently. I reassure them from my own experience. That is my finest qualification for the job: I understand, because I have been there myself.

I have been given my own BBC Radio Wales show, which I broadcast live from St David's Hall in Cardiff twice a year for eight weeks every Friday, before a live audience of six hundred to a thousand people. These are my people, women my age, grannies from the valleys, just like my valley, the Garw. They come down to Cardiff on buses and charabancs. They're my fans, they claim, and I'm theirs.

They look to me to dress as I dress: flowing silk robes from the East with turbans twisted over my hair, which is back to jet-black again. It's not their style, but it's mine. It amuses and interests others, but it succours my soul – the painter in me rejoices to look down at my lap, my arms, my feet, and see so much colour reflecting back at me.

I have recently completed my autobiography, *MOLL: The Making Of Molly Parkin*, published at the same time as an exhibition of my paintings at England & Co., my gallery. I have embarked on the screenplay of this autobiography, commissioned by the American film producer Lionel Rogosin. People ask who will play me. I shrug. 'Who indeed!'

I have grown to love my mature appearance, although I did suffer a loss of physical identity for a few years around the birth of my grandchildren. I allowed my hair to grow out grey, I stopped dyeing it green or red, or blonde, or black, as I had been doing for so many years. Seeing this snow-white, rather distinguished hair was much more of a shock for my friends than for me – until one night in the early hours, returning from the bathroom, I gave myself a severe fright coming face to face with an ashen ghost, a stranger's reflection in the mirror. I no longer recognized myself.

I went for a face-lift. I had the whole works – eyes, chin, everything – and felt restored to myself. I had grown sick of so many people asking me if I was exhausted because I looked it, or unhappy because I appeared so miserable, or irritable over something. Simply the effects of gravity. But more than that in my case – as the cosmetic surgeon explained. I had the prematurely aged face of someone who had abused herself with alcohol, nicotine, a stressful career and broken relationships, and the tensions of an over-whelming ambition which never allowed me any peace. That's what he said. So many ageing factors!

I was thrilled with my face-lift and would recommend one to anybody who, like me, wants to appear as radiant on the surface as she feels inside. I have no hesitation in talking about it if it helps others to make up their own minds, either way. Many women resort to cosmetic surgery – as, indeed, do many men – and feel the need or prefer to keep it a secret. That's all right too. We must all do what we want, behave as it suits us.

That's the conviction I carry today.

My attitude towards men has altered drastically since my bleeding stopped. I have men as friends now, as companions, as true intimates. I no longer regard each as a potential scalp. The entire area of male-female has become what I always longed for it to be instead of the hide-and-seek, tit-for-tat, vicious games-playing that ruled my sexual life.

I have no burning desire for a sexual life, as such, at this time. I have gentlemen callers and male escorts – any number. I love them, really love them all dearly. But my sexuality, as I knew it, simmers now at a very low burn. My sister claims that's not normal, but she is still with the first and only husband she has ever known. It makes a difference, I think. My daughters and other younger women cajole me into asking the Universe for a lover to sweep me off my feet. They, I know, would like to see me with one close male companion for my declining years. I laugh. Who knows what is in store? My *raison d'être* no longer depends on having devoted lovers eating their hearts out over me. I prefer relationships on an equal and easy plateau now, with nothing more demanding than a good-night kiss, knowing I can snuggle under my duvet on my own.

My most exciting love affair currently is with myself, a companion who never fails to astound me with each fresh and absorbing revelation. And because of this I glow, I am a beacon to everyone who meets me. The fact is that the sap no longer rises as it used to do, that my heart no longer palpitates in the presence of a male sex symbol, that my afternoons in the cinema on my own with an ice cream are my genuine idea of fun, more than holding hands in the back row. Even so, I recently took the situation to my doctor, who has put me on hormone replacement therapy which, I am assured, will make some difference. Interesting! We'll see!

The fact that all my talents have been restored to me in

fuller measure than before the chaos burned them to the ground – that is enough for the present. That, and the pride in being taken at a serious level in my writing and painting, the outcome of taking myself seriously.

Miracles must be savoured one by one, as they appear, before the space can be cleared for more. That's what my calm, trusting, post-menopausal self says, this unshakeable self which affords me such joy. Last summer I spent time painting at Craig-Y-Nos Castle in Wales. My grandmother was reared for part of her childhood in this castle, before the family lost it through accumulated debts. I was meant, I knew, to be there with the ghost of this grave and lovely woman, my grandmother. I was blessed by the experience, and felt myself grow.

One afternoon I set off up the steep mountain opposite the castle, hoping to walk all the while with the sun on my face. But I had left it too late: the sun was already sinking. I hurried to catch up with it, taking the stiff gradient in long strides which pulled the breath from my body. Looking above, I could see the upper slopes in sunshine, but never where I was. I laboured in frustration until I reached the very top, not stopping once even to check the view. I was determined to bask in that sun, to feel its warmth, if it was the last thing I did.

Eventually, I got there. The climb had afforded me no pleasure at all. I had failed to notice the bright ferns, the purple heather, the yellow gorse, the rich texture of the black coal-earth. But right at the end, at the very top, I found it all: a view so spectacular that the tears rose in my throat. The clouds so close that I could brush them with my palms. And a sunset so crimson, so pink, so scarlet, so hot on my body, that all I could do was to stretch my arms in celebration.

That was the prize at the end of the climb. 'Like my life,' I shouted, laughing up at the light.

Mitch Cleary

MENOPAUSE WALTZ
Sue O'Sullivan

It wasn't as if she woke up one day and it was gone. Not at all. There were literally years of taking leave, and it was never straightforward. Even now, at fifty-one, when she hadn't seen a drop of red on her knickers for three or four years, its effects lingered: a hot flush here and there; a low-down ache in her gut which took her by surprise before she remembered it wouldn't come again. Over thirty years of bleeding, and then the wind-down and final dribble. She realized there was no way to tell a menopausal tale without a menstrual story.

She had never been one of those women who loved their periods. As a child – and she had been only nine when it started: initially excited, rushing into her parents' bedroom in the early morning of its first appearance – her mother's spontaneous reaction dampened things considerably: 'Oh dear, I am sorry. You're so young.' Still, looking back, she was pretty sure that even if her mother had swept her up in pride, gushing, 'Now you are a woman,' she would have seen the truth before long.

When her periods started coming regularly, from about the age of ten, she experienced a monthly cycle which often included at least one day of heavy, hot, aching cramps, and a week of bleeding into bulky disposable towels which had to be saved in paper bags in her closet and then taken out to the incinerator and burned. She meticulously tied up each used towel and wrapped it in miles of toilet paper – these tight, bloody knots took hours to burn, her cross to bear. What fun was it, and how could she be pleased about the fact that every month she inevitably bled through, at least once, on to her knickers, and had to soak them in cold water, rub salt on to them, scrub them, and still have light tan stains left in the crotch? In her teen years, on her heaviest days, she was known to stuff two – or, in desperation, even three – Kotex down her knickers, or into the special rubber-crotched pants her mother bought her.

Sometimes the cramps were agony. Her mother was of the get-up-and-go school. She rarely communicated any sisterly commiseration, which possibly meant she didn't experience the kind of pain her daughter did. She had a little green-and-white-striped terrycloth-covered electric pad which the girl would go to bed with, holding it to her tummy, fantasizing about a long wooden spoon, wrapped round with cool, wet cotton, which dipped into her and scooped out the dark pool of clotty liquid that lay like poison in her belly. When something was planned by her parents, and she had already spent a half-hour or so curled up with the hot pad, her mother would call her, telling her to get ready to go out, claiming that if she would just get up and start to do something it would feel better. As a result, more than once, she lay in misery, brutish and rolling rhythmically, in the back of the station wagon, while her parents and brothers swam or picnicked.

No, she knew it was not a good thing, although she quickly understood it was the way of things. Her mother was modern in the 1950s sense of the word. She never suggested that there was anything about menstruation to be proud of, but then she never called it the curse either. No, it was something to get used to, to try to ignore as much as possible. Keep busy. Be active. That would take your mind off any little discomfort.

Somewhere along the line, the girl became obsessively concerned that her father or her brothers – or any man, for that matter – might guess that she had her period. Nothing was to be said by her mother. But she could never quite trust her to guard this secret. She wanted her mother to understand without having to tell her. But her mother was careless about her feelings and often seemed oblivious to her distress as she dropped hints that the girl was acting oddly because she had her period. Agonies of burning shame and embarrassment. In high school she worried every single month about bleeding through on to the back of her skirt. She worried about smelling. She worried about starting somewhere without access to a Kotex. All these things happened.

The truth was that after so many years of bleeding every month, she did get used to it. Life went on. She was generally a happy girl, with lots of friends and a good sense of humour. She was blessed with a good 1950s American-style diet, a lot of fresh country air, plenty of exercise, and an urge towards nonconformity. Fucking didn't happen until she was eighteen, so for most of her teenage years she kissed and petted and rolled around with boys fully, or at least partially, dressed. No worries about contraception then, or waiting with baited breath for a period to arrive, but what did you do about a boy feeling the heavy wodge of Kotex as you pressed your clothed bodies together?

Fucking brought new menstrual worries – more concerned with how you told someone you had your period when they wanted to root around down there than with the possibility of getting pregnant. One time she didn't say anything, and he, an older man, removed her pants and her Kotex, and proceeded to fuck her without realizing that she still had a tampon in. She never said a word, but it was hard getting hold of it after it had been banged up inside. Tampons had become possible only after experiencing intercourse. Before that she hadn't been able to get one in, practically fainting in the toilet stall at school with the effort of unsuccessfully poking and pushing about.

Somewhere along the way she picked up that her period pains would improve after she got married. Then, as she got older, she understood that meant after she had a baby. Fortunately, periods did not play a role in her decision to get married or have babies, although she did end up doing both. She fell in love with a British boy and became an American living abroad. She also spent six years on the Pill, which got rid of cramps, got rid of heavy bleeding, prevented conception, but made her feel bloated and strange.

After two babies, living in London, she threw away the Pill for good, tried the coil, which created blood baths from hell, and finally got sterilized. Pregnancy had brought the first disruption of her regular periods. As she settled back to normal it was clear that her cycle was changing, as was the world. Women's liberation arrived in the late 1960s, hot from its American successes. She was captivated, enchanted, transfixed. She was in the midst of her drudge years – all lank long hair, sleepless baby-filled nights and identity crisis. Now, with other women, she discussed many things, including women's bloody cycles. She could see clearly how menstruation's meaning, and even some of the ways it was experienced, arose from what they began to call conditioning. It fascinated her; menstrual stories revealed so much about how girls became women, about fear and loathing, about the female body, about sexuality, about difference.

But she could never make the existential leap into totally accepting and adoring her periods. Embarrassment and shame might be the result of conditioning, but bleeding would happen, happy or sad. She cringed at the new matriarchists who wanted to reclaim menstruation, celebrate it and even – oh my God – dabble in it, adorn their faces with it, drip it across city pavements and country fields. Symbolic or literal, either way it didn't sit well, it didn't strike a note of recognition. It was ridiculous. Menstrual blood was sticky on the thighs if it flowed unplugged. It smelled – sorry, but it did – if it was left on a pad in the warmth. Of course she wanted to change attitudes to menstruation – the attitude of girls who would bleed, her own, men's, and society's. But she wanted nothing to do with locating women's possibilities and powers so firmly in their biology.

She fell in love with a woman, and with lesbian sex. So besotted with making love to women was she that even their blood didn't stand in her way. Now, all these years later, she took her mother's advice and plunged in, keeping busy, letting passion transcend any worry, licking and tasting, and finding it not at all displeasing. To think that the man in her life had told her for so long that it didn't matter to him if she was bleeding and she never really believed him, and certainly never talked about her periods with him.

Periods became a small part of her woman-orientated life. Lovers shared the intimacies of bodies and wondered if, by living together, their cycles were synchronizing, like nuns' did. Fucking with a bleeding lover was one thing; sharing all these details made her go queasy. She might be compelled by her own bloody discharge, but that didn't mean she felt the same way about her girlfriend's. Why did lesbians have to talk about bleeding all the time? It seemed that every time you got together someone was menstruating, feeling pre-menstrual, having period pains, or suffering from something related to it. Every serious lover she had had terrible period problems, and she was expected (and fully expected herself) to be commiserating and sympathetic. In fact she was much better at telling and listening to menstrual stories than at coping with blood clots themselves.

In her late thirties her cycles were changing again. This time, after about six months, she realized something different was beginning: her period was more irregular, and the cycle was getting shorter and shorter. She wondered to herself if this was part of a changing pattern leading to the menopause. Could it be? Wasn't it kind of early? No one else her age brought up the subject. The more she read about the menstrual cycle, the more she realized that there was no clearly defined thing called the menopause. It seemed rare for anyone to be pre-menopausal one moment and post-menopausal the next. The fact was that this process might take years and years to complete.

In the early 1980s she attended an international women's health conference in Switzerland. She went to a workshop on the menopause run by one of the original American *Our Bodies Ourselves* collective members, who eloquently approached the subject with a fan in her hand. She came away from that workshop imagining legions of hot flushing women, willing to whip out their fans in offices, parks, on the streets, in cinemas, recklessly declaring to the world their bloody crisis, perhaps even delighting in it. She fantasized herself as such a woman, and found pleasure in it. But it still felt a long way off.

By the time she was forty-three she began to experience the odd hot flush. What a peculiar sensation! The first time it happened was in public on her own. She felt like a little girl, dying to tell someone, turn to the next person she saw and say, 'My God, you know what's happening to me?' The sweat poured down between her breasts, and her face blushed steamily. And then it was gone, a matter of a thirty-second hormonal eruption. And it wasn't really bad. In fact she decided that it was a little like New York City summer heat: the more you fought against it, the worse it became. The only thing to do was to surrender yourself to it totally, let it flow through you. She began to imagine herself as the menopausal lady, taking London by storm with an out-spoken acknowledgement of her condition. During the day her more modest acts were limited to flinging the windows of the office open, joking that it was another hot flush and she simply had to have air! She bought a beautiful blue Chinese fan, but at the appropriate moment it wasn't always easy to find at the bottom of her work-filled bag.

She was living on her own by now, leaving boys, home, and best-friend husband to sleep like a baby in a tiny, courtyard-facing, noisy, short-life flat in King's Cross. She was besotted with her small estate and, after the first shock of being on her own, enamoured of that condition. Her life felt filled with possibility and a good amount of pleasure. She found her forties her most fulfilling decade yet. At the same time, she had some pretty spectacular relationship failures which left her curled in a ball on the floor sobbing through the nights, but in the end she recovered. Once, when the loss and betrayal and grief turned the world grey for a couple of months, she felt compelled to find a shrink, something she had never thought would be necessary or right for her. It was, and it worked, and she changed a tiny bit.

After six months or so of hot flushing, just as she was really getting serious about it all, the daytime flushes went, disappeared, vanished. The nighttime soaks remained – usually not extreme, but sometimes occurring up to ten or twelve times a night. The first time it had happened, with her lover lying there beside her, she felt embarrassed, but the woman was intrigued and interested. She was – as all her lovers had been – younger, and certainly not meno-pausal. They discovered that sex and flushes often went together, and that a good session of snogging could bring a little one on. Her girlfriend got blasé and was prone to say things like 'Having a little flush, then, Susie?' which, while comforting, was occasionally irritating.

She told everyone she was menopausal, including her mother, who denied it. 'No,' said her mother, 'you aren't.' In a perfect continuation of their relationship, she found herself defensively arguing yes, it was happening to her, as if perhaps she was the one who had made a mistake. Then she decided to let it pass. Other people believed her, although they usually told her she was too young or went glazed in the eyes and pretended their attention was demanded elsewhere.

She wrote a secret poem called 'Menopause Waltz' in which her ambivalences were expressed. She didn't dread the loss of her bloody cycle, but she did worry about getting a dried-up cunt. That, more than anything else, nagged and made her apprehensive. It was hard to admit, because somehow it seemed self-obsessed and vaguely unimportant. But in fact, here she was, relatively late in life, getting off on slick vaginal secretions, sliding-sweet, sexy-wet. Her own and others'. Feeling sexual meant getting wet; getting wet meant fingers could open her up, and wanting more. Wanting more meant asking for it harder, and more and more. Getting sucked and licked was the best thing ever for fantastic orgasms, but fucking with a woman was different and amazing. Even if you were in a fantasy at home on your own, it was nice to reach down and push in and feel how warm and smooth and wet you were. Was this going to be lost? The descriptions were not reassuring: thinning vaginal walls, atrophied vagina, dry, possibly sore, cunts. Dreadful. It didn't seem to be happening at all during the menopausal process, but what about later?

It was double-edged, starting the menopause early. It worried her when people told her she looked too young to be menopausal, because although she was a bit flattered, she then wondered what people would think when, inevitably, she did look old. Having never been particularly attached to her periods but being a worry-wort, she also puzzled that perhaps she was being a bit offhand about their loss. It was true that the few years of change had made her more interested in the real bloody discharge, more attentive to its smell, look and texture. When it was truly gone, would she have some sort of psychic crisis? Claiming that personally it had nothing substantial to do with feeling complete as a woman might be a huge denial. God, sometimes she wished she hadn't dabbled in psychoanalytic chit chat.

She kept a menstrual chart through all of her forties and that was how she finally figured out it was gone for good and that she was post-menopausal. It was quite a shock to realise that more than two years had gone by since her last period, because she still thought of herself as being in some sort of process. She remembered the series of dreams – they must have happened in the first year of an absence of blood. Each time she was sitting on the toilet; each time she reached down, tissue in hand, and came up with red stained paper. Each time she woke up feeling incredibly sad and then as consciousness returned, incredibly relieved.

There were no tampons in her flat; she had thrown away the last of them and expected her lover to provide her own. She rarely thought about periods. It felt entirely natural not to have them. No, more than natural, it felt wonderful. No mess, no fuss, no pain, no stains, no smell of warm blood, no lower gut ache or loosening of the bowels. Goodbye to all that.

She still had hot flushes at least a couple of times a week. She still felt the ebb and flow of bodily changes which seemed to be steered by hormonal patterns. Her emotions had never been at the total beck and call of her physiological processes, but they were still gratifyingly inconsistent, surprising and pleasurable. But this happened without the inconvenience of one whole bloody week a month taken up with periods. It was fantastic when she realised how absolutely freeing it was.

At the same time she also realised that she felt considerably distanced and uncaring about other women's periods. She did try to be polite and interested when the conversation turned to who was having what sort of period. She made the right noises when a woman friend or lover complained of bad pains or something associated with menstruation. But really it was like trying to hark back to the Dark Ages. Of course it wasn't their fault. She certainly wasn't suggesting, if only to herself, that they should all go out and get hysterectomies. No, she wouldn't even have joked that way. It was more feeling sorry for them, but also feeling as if she'd done her time, it had had its moments and served its purpose, but now she was leaving it behind.

Her current and steadiest ever lover, still in her thirties and regular as clockwork, was not one of her complaining companions. But she suspected that even she noticed her lack of interest. More difficult was the recognition that she wasn't really keen to fuck with her beloved when she was bleeding. In her thirties and much of her forties, she had spent a lot of time as a women's health activist and writer, talking with women about overcoming their self-disgust, their dislike of their own and other women's monthly bleeding. Oh, she could hear the times she had said, 'It's not dirty. There is nothing wrong with having sex when you are menstruating. You may find you feel randy then.' She had gently prodded women to engage with their partners' dislike of or ambivalence about their blood, and tell them if they were interested in sex at that time. In the past her own husband had communicated to her that he was not turned off at all by her bleeding and would engage in any sexual acts that she wanted during that time. She realized now that he had been more accepting than she was.

Back in the seventies and early eighties she had been aware of feminist critiques of hormone replacement therapy. She had been part of the women's health movement, taught women's health in Holloway Prison, gained a diploma in Health Education, and finally ended up at *Spare Rib* magazine, where she was responsible for most of the health articles for the five years she stayed on the collective. She wasn't a hardliner about health care; if the menopause drove you nuts and made you miserable and HRT helped, she wasn't going to come on all judgemental. But she did think it was strange that after all the criticisms, all the exposés of how profit-driven and blandly disinterested in women drug companies were, anyone could merrily leap on the HRT bandwagon. Then there were the revolting paeans to the magical effects HRT had on women's ability to stay youthful and beautiful, with smooth faces and elastic cunts. When possible dangers associated with HRT began to come to light, it didn't surprise her at all.

Memories are short, time flies by, and drug companies are loath to give up. By the end of the eighties HRT was making a comeback, only now osteoporosis was the buzz word, striking terror in women's hearts. Suddenly every woman she knew was nervous about brittle bones, wondering if they too would end up cracking hips, developing dowager's humps, breaking wrists. Surely HRT was the answer – and, not only that, it dampened hot flushes and made women feel happy! Several of her contemporaries who were not even menopausal asked her if she was on HRT when she talked about her menopause. When she answered no, they asked, 'Why not?' To which she replied, 'Why?'

Why should she if she didn't find the flushes impossible, wasn't depressed, felt energetic and didn't believe HRT was the only way to stay fit and healthy? Thinking it over, she decided the subtext was almost always a fear of growing old, looking older. Strange that feminists, so confident in their more youthful twenties and thirties about the ephemeral nature of 'attractiveness', and its male-defined meanings, began to waver and lose confidence in their forties and fifties. Sad and understandable, but maddening. She wasn't immune – especially alone, at night. The more women she heard extolling the wonders of HRT with breathy sideways remarks about how good they felt – glowing skin, springy cunts – the more she wondered gloomily if she was making some sort of silly stand. Would she regret it in ten years' time? Then she would catch herself and think how ridiculous, she didn't look any different from the women who took HRT, she didn't need to medicalize her perfectly normal changes, she didn't have to bury the signals of change in her life. She had always celebrated change. Why stop now? She had no more reason to trust drug companies today than she had ten years ago. The difference now was that she didn't have a group of peers meeting together regularly to talk about their lives, committed to discovering the social roots of their private fears and confusions. She wasn't really hankering after those old days, but it helped to remember them.

In the last year or so, as she became more and more post-menopausal, she noticed more signs of ageing in herself. Were they connected to being post-menopausal, or were they happening because she was – older? Did it really matter? Her cunt was a little less wet. By this time she was deeply involved in AIDS work, running workshops and writing a lot for women about sex, sexuality, and safer sex. Familiarity with safer-sex techniques meant getting relaxed about lubricants. Lubes and latex go together like a horse and carriage. Her ex-lover in San Francisco sent her a plastic bottle of Probe, a water-based lube. It was wonderful. No more greasy gunk. What had seemed an admission of defeat, of sometimes needing help, of loss of spontaneity, was transformed into matter-of-factness and pleasure.

She thought, finally, that the menopause was a wonderful thing. It gave women a clear hint of their mortality, and if they were receptive, it gave them a chance to reflect on their life. For her it was a signpost of change, and signalled that she had completed the longest period of her life. She read Germaine Greer on the menopause, and wished that many other women could tell their tales as widely. For her the change was not about accepting a loss of sexual engagement, nor did she believe that lesbians necessarily experienced menopause in the same way as Greer claimed heterosexual women did. But she agreed wholeheartedly with her that any wishful desire for 'no change' was desperately sad and horrible.

She felt differently passionate, differently engaged, differently but happily a woman, now that she was free of menstruation. She could still be blue and get depressed, but those were not conditions which typified her life. She could be deeply serious and self-sufficient at times, and laugh till her sides ached with a bunch of girlfriends at others. She could be pleased with her memories, filled with love for her grown-up children, and still fizz with expectation at a new idea for work or relaxation. She wept and raged at the grotesque levels of suffering and exploitation in the world, but she still considered herself committed to being part of changing that. She was sometimes confused and troubled by the end-of-the-century political scene, but she was confident in a way she had never been when she was younger. She was still the queen of second-hand shopping and still intended to get fit, but she fully understood that some possibilities were in the past for her. Each decade of her life had spun itself out at the time as the best. She saw no reason to think the next few wouldn't continue the tradition. Now if only she could shed those extra post-menopausal pounds . . .

A NEW BEGINNING
Doreen Asso

Like most people, probably, my feelings and views about
the menopause are not simple; a kaleidoscope of impressions
emerges from many years of research, teaching, and counselling with women. In my family the menopause was
rarely referred to directly, and it was never discussed openly
or at any length. There were occasional murmurings about
'going through' something, with the implication that it
wasn't good.

Later, a scientific training greatly influenced me in my
expectations of – and attitudes to – the menopause, in three
broad ways: first, research findings, mostly based on
women's own reports, quite simply refute many of the
things which are said about the menopause and its effects.
Secondly, some understanding of the events of the whole
life cycle and the relative importance of the menopause
within it gives a different view. Thirdly, the work now

being done on biological and other, external, cycles provides a much wider perspective. Less scientifically, the counselling I do gives me an opportunity to see some women experiencing the menopause at first hand. There were also, as for most people, friends of similar age or ahead of me who influenced my feelings.

All these sources of information counteracted the images created by folklore and by the media, and I will try to show how they influenced my experience of the menopause, and how they might do the same for others.

The ending of the reproductive cycle is a subject which generates an endless preoccupation with the loss of fertility and the proclaimed onset of old age, bone loss, increased psychological problems and decline in sexuality. Yet apart from the formal ending of fertility, these things do not happen suddenly – if they happen at all – with the menopause, and they also happen in men.

The preoccupation with decline specifically in women cannot be laid only at the door of men; many women writers and commentators present the same ideas. The messages from the media and elsewhere leave some women marvellously untouched; others may absorb them and even repeat them, but their own experience, whether positive or negative, seems to be unique to them, regardless. Women, in the end, are not as gullible as some suppose, and most of us manage the fluctuations of the menstrual cycle and its end pretty well, despite the images of doom which are perpetuated. It is the effect on other people of partial and erroneous information which can be so powerful.

I would like to suggest how thinking about this particular transition might be changed by calling on three main sources (research evidence; greater awareness of the whole life cycle; some understanding of other cycles) to put the menopause into a more accurate, positive and broader framework which might have considerable individual and social implications. I hope this piece will not seem arid and academic; it's about the real feelings of women, in the wider universe in which they live; it's about the possibility of doing away with wrong impressions and outdated ideas, and replacing them with more constructive ones. This is a good time, in the middle of a social revolution in attitudes to 'a woman's place' and the ageing of men and women, for a reappraisal of the potential within each person, of either sex, at any time in their lives.

Let's start with the women themselves, and what they actually say in carefully conducted studies whose aim is to provide unbiased and representative information on a subject which has been — and often still is – misunderstood. As women pass their first youth and start to accomplish the different phases of their lives, they begin to feel more positive about the ending of their reproductive years. Although they do not look forward to any discomfort or distress that may come with it, over the years, and nearer and during the time of the menopause, their view of the whole process changes. By the time they are middle-aged and actually experiencing pre-menopausal and menopausal changes, and then pass through the post-menopausal era, the majority speak of being more confident, calmer and freer than before; a bonus comes with maturity and experience. They do not see the menopause as a discontinuity, and they believe that women can have – or can be given – a degree of control over their symptoms. Also, they see this time as more positive for themselves than for other women; they perceive other women (but not themselves) more in the light of the stereotypes which have become so tenacious. Even so, in general, negative stereotypes are less prevalent among women than among men. Many of these stereotypes are fed by mistaken attribution of symptoms to the menopause when in fact their origins are elsewhere: the normal ageing process, common to everyone; pre-existing problems and symptoms; and events that are quite unrelated to menopause.

If we look at women's feelings about specific aspects of the menopause, there are some surprises. The end of fertility, far from being dreaded, is welcomed, and this is true of women of various cultures: traditional Muslim Arabs, Turks, Persians, North Africans, and women from Western Europe; as one of my colleagues has written, quoting from Ecclesiastes, it seems that for women 'To everything there is a season'. Then we hear a lot about the emotional impact on women of the departure of children and the collapse of their usefulness and happiness that goes with that. The careful studies show that this does not provoke symptoms or a loss of well-being in the great majority; some (rare) women who have overprotective and overinvolved relationships with their children do suffer, but this is not usual, and any suffering comes *whenever* the child leaves home, which is often several years before or after the menopausal age of fifty. Relationships with partners can be strained through the menopausal transition, but the problems are usually long-standing, and although they may be exacerbated by the menopause, they do not in general start with it.

The fact is that the only significant factor which is associated with an increase in psychological symptoms (over and above pre-existing ones) during the menopausal years is linked with work. Underprivileged, low socioeconomic groups are most likely to have an increase in symptoms. The effects of working or not working are complex: work seems to be beneficial to women in higher socioeconomic groups, but less so – and sometimes even harmful – to the less privileged others, probably because of the strain of combining running a family and a home with what is often a physically demanding job. In general the findings show that across the range of cultural and religious groups, the women who enjoy high levels of well-being through the menopause are either those who have more opportunities to seek satisfaction outside the home, coping with and enjoying the changes in the life cycle, or traditional women with a central role in the household. It is those who are caught in the middle, in times of rapid cultural change, who have most difficulty in adapting to the menopause.

Wherever we look, the idea that there is a particular psychological syndrome linked to the menopause, over and above the problems which may exist or occur at any time in life, simply has no solid backing. Apart from initially symptom-free bone loss, which predisposes to osteoporosis much later on, the two hormonally related symptoms are hot flushes and a dry vagina. These symptoms can be distressing and demoralizing, and can affect sleep, work, sexual enjoyment and one's whole outlook on life; if they are alleviated, any secondary psychological effects disappear or are lessened. For the rest, there is no evidence of supposed psychological problems in the menopausal phase. It turns out that the incidence of psychological difficulties at menopause is, if anything, somewhat less than at certain other times. One reliable study found the highest levels of psychological symptoms in the age range thirty-five to forty-four (which is not even the pre-menopause); afterwards they declined. Another study also found that the peak for frank mental disorders was these ages, after which there was a decrease. A comprehensive study of women of all ages found no increase with age (including the menopausal transition) of a range of psychological symptoms investigated, and in fact found a *decline*, with age, of headaches and irritability. Another survey also found that irritability declined significantly in women at about the age of forty-eight, whereas it did not decline in men.

The claims about the psychological havoc wrought by

loss of fertility, loss of useful occupation, and loss of sexuality have no sound basis. The facts about fertility through the reproductive years give a view which is rather different from the usual one about the abrupt ending of fertility. In several good studies, women who were asked about positive as well as negative effects reported the ending of the reproductive years not as a loss to be mourned, but as a time of well-being and of a different kind of unencumbered enjoyment and fulfilment. The other two great stereotypes which are assumed to be psychologically damaging – loss of a useful occupation and loss of sexuality – are easy to dispel. Of course we cannot underestimate the importance of the satisfactions and rewards of family and home, and of work (and those deprived of work know this only too well); but for most people this does not end at fifty, and it is misguided to think that it is lost with the menopause. Women who have made family and home their main occupation continue to be interested in homemaking, and most have the new and joyous prospect of grandchildren; also, they are good at finding other interests and occupations, which they are well able to do at fifty. Those who work outside the home could all be helped (and occasionally are) to plan more constructively, in advance, for retirement – whether from work in, or out of, the home. As for sexuality, the implication that women's sexuality declines more than that of men is wrong; rather the contrary: men are more vulnerable, for more reasons, to decline. In women, provided that vaginal dryness is dealt with (and there are a number of effective treatments, both hormonal and non-hormonal), sexual desire follows a similar pattern to that of men – there is a gradual lessening in quantity, but not necessarily in the amount of pleasure. Loss of libido is not primarily a result of hormonal changes; for the same reason, oestrogen therapy does not have a significant primary effect on libido. Attraction is not only about obvious sex appeal, but about a spark of real interest, rising alertness, and a stirring of a physical as well as an intellectual buzz. The immediate pigeonholing of people on the grounds of age, for whatever purpose, reflects a misunderstanding of the potential in every person for vibrancy, interest, and stimulation throughout the life span.

The published evidence is based on *group* figures. Let us not lose sight, within these group results, of those individuals who experience real psychological distress as a result of hot flushes and/or vaginal dryness, in combination with their past experience and particular life events at the time. But the more carefully conducted studies show that this is not more true (and probably less so) than at some other times in their lives. Through any transitions, especially those involving physical changes, some people experience more distressing psychological manifestations of these changes than others; and this is true of some women in reaction to the menopausal hormonal changes.

Perhaps the disproportionate negative attention given to the menopause tells us something about the need for a different perspective on life. If women themselves feel positive about the menopause, should not the rest of the world think about it more rationally?

There is no justification for the idea of a menopausal state of mind; the end of the reproductive years has wrongly been made a focus for problems and reactions which happen in various forms at any time of life, and happen equally to men throughout their lives. Men and women certainly have to adapt, eventually, to the ending of their working lives, and to finding meaningful ways of spending their time; and, at some point, of dealing with problems of ageing and declining powers. None of these challenges is related to the menopause, and they come later than fifty.

Why, then, does the idea persist of specific psychological problems connected with the menopause? The most obvious reasons seem to be as follows: a lot of studies were done on women who were attending gynaecological clinics for various reasons; it is known that women with psychological problems frequently seek help at gynaecological clinics, so these clinic-attenders are not typical of most menopausal women. For the same reason, clinicians often assume a causal relationship between the menopause and psychological problems. In the past there may have been a rather stronger basis for the supposed psychological symptoms; this is now changing as clinicians become more aware, and more effective treatments become available. The folklore (still powerful) is based on the idea that the most important – and, in some cultures, the sole – purpose of life for women is to bear and nurture children. It seems that as a society evolves it begins to be accepted that women have fulfilment needs other than solely those of having children. Certainly, in our society, the lives of most women are changing, more choices are open to at least some of them, and many expect – and are expected – to contribute a good deal more than childbearing. And, as I have said, the studies show that most women do not regret the ending of their reproductive years.

The second source of a changed perspective is in thinking about the human life cycle as a whole. Within the life span, the processes of the decline in fertility and in sexuality, and of ageing, take place over a great many years. The thirty-seven potentially reproductive years occupy less than half of the average expected life span for a woman. Within those years, every cycle is not ovulatory; around 25 per cent of cycles in young women are anovulatory, and ovulation declines steadily from about the age of forty onwards. Peak fertility lasts for about twenty years, between the ages of twenty and forty, and during the seven years of menopausal transition conception is extremely unlikely. Of all conceptions over the age of forty, 40 per cent are terminated, for various reasons, and this is surely more distressing than the expected ending of menstruation and fertility. Also, most women in the West choose to have children on only two or three occasions in the course of their reproductive years; for the rest of the thirty-seven years, each monthly cycle ends in abrupt reversal of the reproductive process – a reversal which is often very difficult for a few days, and the ending of which is one of several benefits of the menopause.

Men also have a steady decline in fertility from at least the age of forty, for several possible reasons: levels of testosterone, which are related to the amount of sexual behaviour; decline with age, on average (with wide individual differences) from around forty onwards; there is a marked decline in penile sensitivity with age, usually before forty, and with this decline in sensitivity of the penis comes a decrease in amount of sexual intercourse; impotence in men starts to increase sharply after the age of forty, and reaches a peak in the fifties and onwards. So the decline in fertility is gradual, and characteristic of both men and women.

More generally, there are developmental changes throughout the whole of the life span, and these start to become slightly more marked, in both men and women, from about the age of forty. The menopause cannot be seen as a marker for the beginning of old age; a woman of fifty in the West has an average life expectancy of just over thirty years: more than a third of her life still to live. (Men of fifty have an average life expectancy of just over twenty-five years.) Everyone, male and female alike, loses bone after forty, though the loss is more gradual in men than in women.

It is hard to see why, in popular as well as specialist minds, the climacteric in women has been singled out so much more than many other transitions and developmental stages which take place throughout the course of every human life. Each of these stages (puberty, becoming a husband, wife, mother or father) can give both joys and new difficulties, but we see them as part of our common existence, and no persistently negative image attaches to them. I believe that for the increasing number of women who, like me, work regularly, the ending of menstruation will not be seen or felt as different from other transitions. Even the physical symptoms, apart from the hot flushes, are not outside the realm of common experience and can, with or without help, be managed, as are any other symptoms experienced by anyone through life.

The third source of perspective is the growing understanding of the whole range of cycles which are constantly affecting us. In the continual activity of all these naturally occurring rhythms, endings and beginnings are virtually indistinguishable. Feelings, behaviour, alertness, and other psychological and physical states are all subject to continual rhythmic activity, from within the individual and from outside forces. These cycles – from the repetitive firing of single nerve fibres to the one great developmental cycle from conception to death – are always interacting with the constant movement of the earth and the moon, the sun, and other cosmic forces, to produce more or less subtle influences on every aspect of existence.

This is not just the province of biology or physics or astrology. We can all benefit from knowing more about the interplay between cycles within and outside the individual. Cosmic movements determine the internal rhythms of each one of us through electromagnetic radiation. Jet lag, for instance, is the result of individual body rhythms going out of phase with the relative positions of the earth, the sun and the moon. Another example is the link between the reproductive and lunar cycles. The length of the lunar cycle is 29.5 days, and so is the average menstrual cycle; and it is when the length of the reproductive cycle most closely equals the length of the lunar cycle that women are most likely to be fertile. Apart from the reproductive cycle, the twenty-four-hour light/dark, circadian cycle is probably the most obvious one, but most of us are not fully aware of its effects, which are fundamental and far-reaching. There are powerful, cyclical, time-of-day effects, for instance, on behaviour, mood, perceptions of self, and so on, and these interact with the other cycles. New evidence about the effects of these various cycles is leading to better ways of turning the many beneficial ones to good account, and preventing or overcoming any bad ones – I shall say more about this below. There are cycles – ultradian, circadian, infradian – in all the internal and behavioural functions, in the developmental and ageing processes, in symptoms. Out there, influencing these internal rhythms, there are cyclical electromagnetic and other geophysical and cosmic movements, rhythms in the sea, the earth, the planets. It is remarkable that in this vast pattern of rhythmic activity we choose to single out the ending of the reproductive cycle in women as a negative event, to be suffered by the women themselves and those around them with brave words and gritted teeth, rather than as another ending of a cycle and the opening up of another era.

Happily, as I have said, most women do not perceive the menopause in this way. The recurring theme, from several different sources, is of a potentially bright future for women at fifty. Of course adaptations are needed, and like other transitions, this one is worth preparing for. Some women, for various reasons, will need more help than others: accurate, understandable information; competent help with any symptoms; and opportunities for talking and planning.

If the menopause is to be more than just an ending, there have to be some choices which open up. The way you spend the last third or more of your life will be partly determined by what has gone before; and many people have not had a great deal of choice in that. Some have been more fortunate, and have had – or been able to find – a wide range of interests, and possibilities for the future. I am struck by the number of choices which are open to me and to many of the people I know in this era of our lives. We are privileged because most of us have interesting work and/or thriving families; we have opportunities to develop our inner resources; and we do not have severe financial worries. None of us feels that the best parts of our life span are over; on the contrary, we feel a release of energy and some added strength from a little more knowledge and experience. It is easy to be positive with these advantages, and the aim has to be to make it possible for all women – and men – to have the support and the inner and other resources to open up new horizons at this potentially wonderful stage of their lives.

This does not happen by just saying it and talking about it, or by some miracle. The right kind of – brief – counselling at this stage can direct women (and men) to ways of developing a sense of all dimensions of themselves, to be aware of their identity as an integral person, more than (but including) children, or work. The struggle for self-realization is often easier once some of the more pressing imperatives are removed; and there is a marvellous openness to personal development in many people at this time of life. I do not see us as menopausal women losing our all – our children, our sexual attractiveness, our energy; or ageing men, past their prime, losing their sexual powers and their hair. This is a human and social issue, not exclusive either to women or to men – it is about the way we see ourselves, and how the rest of the world sees us.

In the process of self-realization a person explores fully his or her needs, searches for greater self-knowledge and for ways of fulfilling important needs and purposes. The psychological, spiritual and physical dimensions must all come into this exploration if we are to become whole, integrated beings. In younger life, often (but not always) there seems to be little time for thinking about our spirituality. Yet most of us feel that there is a dimension beyond the more visible physical and psychological aspects of existence, and that we are part of a wider universe. Some may decide, quite early on, that if there is a spiritual dimension it has to be rejected or ignored as unimportant, unknowable, or whatever; but usually they feel the need to return to the question. With time, spirituality often seems not only more important, but even positively life-enhancing. Many of us go to great lengths to provide for our physical comfort, and neglect our spiritual well-being; but more and more, the powerful properties of contemplation, meditation, and opening up to our spirituality are being integrated into our lives. One of the many benefits which comes with this is a keener sense of proportion and a widening of our thinking, feeling and sensory horizons. All this can be with us from an early age, but for many it comes with time, and from our fifties onwards we can take advantage of the shift away from some activities to areas where an open mind, tolerance and self-honesty are the keys to immensely rewarding realms of experience.

None of this alters the fact that more thought and effort must be given to the minority of women who do suffer considerable distress through the menopause. This distress is absolutely not just the result of 'wrong' thinking, but if there were more general acceptance that the menopause can be a positive event for virtually all women, these women would not be surrounded by the stereotyped images which create forebodings throughout their reproductive years. Pre-menopausal women could have more reliable and more detailed information, clinical advice when needed, and help with developing a sense of perspective, and knowing how to benefit from transitions. There could be more discussion of individual problems; apart from correcting the general misinformation, a formulaic approach does not help much when someone has distressing symptoms. Some of us (and I was one of them) have the advantage of knowing the range of treatments for these symptoms, and their secondary effects; many women do not. Any one approach does wonders for some, but not for others; some influential writers, and some clinicians, press the advantages of one treatment only, as a blanket remedy for everyone. The facts about hormone therapy, for example, could be put more clearly and less dramatically; it is certainly an answer for some people, but not for others, and for many the effects of the seven to twelve days of progestogens can outweigh the benefits. Instead of oversimplified presentations, women need informed advice: whether, for instance, to adopt compromise solutions such as a local hormonal treatment for vaginal dryness, and to use self-help methods to deal with hot flushes and secondary psychological distress. The value of self-help methods is hard to overestimate; they are not always the whole answer, but they can improve the quality of life and, above all, they give each person some control over their discomfort.

New research findings are increasing the potential of relaxation and exercise, for instance, by combining with them a growing understanding of the highly influential effects of biological cycles. Just one example illustrates the ways in which the findings from different areas of research are coming together to improve well-being at any time, and particularly – for our purposes – when change both imposes discomfort and offers new possibilities to be grasped. It has been known for some time that raised arousal in the central nervous system gives feelings of alertness, buoyancy, and positive mood; also that arousal in another nervous system, the autonomic, determines levels of tension, perceived threat, and so on. The levels in these two nervous systems fluctuate systematically with the time of day (that is, they have a circadian cycle); so do their marked effects on feelings and behaviour. We are dimly aware of this, but mostly do not benefit sufficiently from this remarkable intrinsic coping mechanism.

Science is now giving us a further understanding of biological underpinnings of feelings, mood and behaviour which has everyday applications. As central (energetic) arousal and autonomic (tense) arousal rise and fall in a predictable rhythm throughout the day, the fluctuations are subtly influencing our perception of ourselves; of problems; of personal relations; and of social interactions. For instance, following the daily curve of nervous system arousal, we are more optimistic and less tense as the morning progresses; and less optimistic and more tense in the late afternoon. Problems which seem insurmountable late at night appear perfectly manageable in the morning. What is more, we can change the levels of energetic and tense arousal in the two nervous systems by the simplest means. A brisk ten-minute walk increases central arousal, and so increases optimism and positive feelings and reduces tension; and there are several other devices, such as relaxation or meditation, which are highly effective in changing the levels and types of arousal.

With the natural fluctuations in circadian cycles of arousal, we can make best use of the energetic, positive times of day; and we can try to relax, meditate, use positive images or distractor techniques at the low-energy, high-tension times. If we realize the influence of the movement of the earth around the sun, and if we use some simple devices to modify arousal levels, we have ways of feeling and perceiving differently which really work.

The age of fifty is a good time to tune into every aspect of our being as it is at present, but with the perspective of the whole life span; and to become aware of our place in the wider universe. Then we will be able to keep our equanimity if our eyebrows turn grey, and our chin line starts to sag a little. The climate is right: we are living in a time of growing emphasis on the importance of the whole person; also, there is increasing openness to self-help approaches and a greater self-awareness.

I have spoken from personal experience, greatly influenced by my particular education and training. Because of my work and the experiences of friends, the menopause was not a cause for anxiety for me. I expected some discomfort, but not so exceptional that it could not be dealt with. I was immersed in personal, working and social life. My few – and mild – symptoms responded to rather simple measures which had been effective at other times and for other people.

All that I have written here is just one route to more positive feelings. There is a lot more to living a rewarding life, but these are some ways of thinking and feeling about a transition which can – but need not – be especially difficult. Science does not always help with life events, but it gave me the facts about the menopause and a broad context in which to expect and live it. I hope that more self-knowledge, with some help from science and enlightened social policies, will increasingly help everyone to think of the transition from middle to later life as another good ending – and another good beginning.

Nigel Parry

WHEN THE MACHINERY STOPS WORKING

Ursula Owen

I am looking at a photograph of my mother. On the back it says August 1963. She is fifty-four. She is beautiful, rather tentative, looking anxious. Looking her age, they would say – in other words, ageing, which means they have lost interest in you.

I have never talked to my mother about her experience of the menopause, or mine. But I know enough to know how very different it was for her. For a start, her machinery was in better order than mine – she gave birth to three children.

I am used to the machinery not working. If for many women the menopause is the first time they face the fact that they can no longer have children, for me it was only the end of a long line of uncertainties, battles with the body that had been going on since my late twenties.

Gynaecologically, my history has been one of a certain amount of chaos and a good deal of black comedy. In the mid 1960s I wanted to get pregnant and couldn't. Tests for infertility were poorly developed and crude, and almost all doctors were pretty uninterested in the problem, though it was known even then that at least one in ten couples, and probably more, had difficulty conceiving. Various suggestions were made. Perhaps we made love too fast? Did I know about the most fertile periods of the cycle? Was I tense? In cubicles with no tops where everyone heard everyone else's answer, I was asked whether I had orgasms. I was slapped genially on the thigh by young male doctors who said, 'We'll get you pregnant.' (I swear they never understood what they were saying.)

The comedy became farce. We were sometimes required to make love at six o'clock in the morning for a fertility test – rather heroically succeeding on all but one occasion, when we were severely reprimanded for failing and so missing an appointment. And each month I would hold my breath in a state of excitement and tension of a kind never felt before or since, as I waited for the first drops of blood and prayed they wouldn't come – examining my breasts for enlarged veins, looking in my heart for some knowledge beyond the physical facts that would assure me I had joined womanhood.

It is such a particular feeling, this sense that you can't do this most ordinary of things, this thing that seems to happen to people all the time, whether they want it or not. (Later I was to learn that the world is divided into women desperately trying to have babies and women desperately trying not to have them, and that the pain of one is not necessarily worse than the other, as I had always been so sure it was.) Pregnant women at all stages of pregnancy become the most beautiful in the world, the most envied. I thought about little else, while always trying to protect myself against the next disappointment. I decided to address friends who had babies (it was the time when everyone seemed to be having families of four) with huge, exaggerated interest, determined not to be pitied. And always this sense that I was not a proper woman, never had been, never would be. (During that time I often remembered how my classmates at school had insisted I should be barren Calpurnia when we read *Julius Caesar*, because I was the only one whose periods hadn't started yet. The comic brutalities of school life.)

In the mid 1960s there was no women's movement, and being infertile (subfertile, as it turned out; I did manage to get pregnant once, much later) was an even lonelier business than it might have been. I longed for a child – and I was not doing what the world expected of me. When a Jewish girl starts her first period, she is slapped on the cheek and told she is now a woman. There are many versions of this, in many cultures. In ours it's perhaps less ritualized, but any woman who has not had a child, for whatever reason, knows how she is seen. Question: when is a woman not a woman? Answer: when she's not a mother. A curious and revealing equation, come to think of it, for a culture which decides that when we are young, and menstrual, we are unwomanly if we don't have children; when we are older, and menopausal, we are unwomanly because we can't have children; and when we are mothers, we are marginalized.

I could hardly fail to be aware of the pitfalls of this particular social construction of womanliness, and it became necessary for survival to try to resist the influence of my physiology on my self-image, including my sexual self-image. I learned to be robust, raucous about my body. I was determined not to go under. And somehow, despite the stereotypes of the infertile woman, I did not, during this time, feel unsexual or undesirable. Who knows why? No doubt sheer necessity did its bit.

Whatever it was, this early experience of battling with

the image of failure, of unwomanliness in the eyes of the world, seems to have given me a particular view of the menopause. To me it doesn't seem this dramatic moment of change, this milestone of ageing, of utterly changed self-image, of huge loss. All those things have happened more gradually to me. And keeping sexuality and fertility separate has become something of a habit over time.

In fact, the menopause itself turned out to be more complicated. True to form, my poor battered womb, never doing quite what it should, developed fibroids so enormous that in the end, after a ten-year delay, a good deal of pain, and politically as well as personally correct efforts to avoid it, I had to have a hysterectomy. (The fibroids filled a bucket, so let no one persuade you that it's always better to avoid hysterectomy. I nearly wrecked various organs of the body by delaying so long.)

That was at the age of forty-seven. The menopause proper came later, at fifty-four: mildish physical symptoms – certainly mild compared with those of some of my friends. I had already felt some of the effects of not having periods (or a womb) long before the hormonal changes began. And by the time I had a hysterectomy I had grieved so much for my malfunctioning womb that I felt almost pure relief at the end of pain.

Not that the menopause isn't still quite hard to write about. One feels a kind of tired fatalism about putting one's head on the block. It is surely asking for trouble, isn't it, to admit you're having the menopause, living those 'silent, secret years'? Part of the difficulty is that we know so little about it. As Germaine Greer points out in her brilliant, wonderfully readable book: 'It is only our ignorance which implies that all menopausal women are enduring the same trials and responding in the same way.'

As usual, when the male establishment isn't very interested in something, it pretends it doesn't exist. It's no accident, of course, that so little has been known even about the physical symptoms of the menopause, let alone emotional, psychological, spiritual changes. Invisibility is something women are used to, and there's no woman as invisible as a post-menopausal woman. Yet even when women write about it, so much of the talk about how ageing women are marginalized revolves round sexuality. A much-loved aunt, a spirited woman, devout Quaker, committed socialist, told me at the age of sixty how awful it felt not to be looked at as an attractive woman any more. I remembered the pain and passion with which she said it, thirty years later. It's true – that's more or less how it is still, though not always so totally or categorically as some claim. Women do live lives where their ageing bodies are loved, or continue to be loved. Let's not be soft on sexism, or ageism, but let's not exaggerate. There might, after all, be the odd prospect of happy fucks for the ageing body. The last thing we need is to create a new form of political correctness for the older woman.

I have examined that tentative look of my mother's in the photograph so closely, so often. Hesitant though I am to say it in this continuingly misogynist society, I think that for some of my generation the experience of ageing is a little different. Women in their mid-fifties now sometimes encounter the odd, rather backhanded compliment: 'You can't be . . . It's impossible . . .' They may smile a little in response, not ungratefully. This is the first generation of women where at least the luckier ones are not considered to be on the scrapheap after the menopause, have not become more or less invisible or irrelevant once the machinery has stopped working.

What has made the difference? I don't think the sexual liberations of the past thirty years have much altered women's experience of ageing. 'It's every woman's tragedy that, after a certain age, she looks like a female impersonator,' Angela Carter once said. But I think two things *have* changed: women's place in the world of work, the marketplace; and a change in the breadth and possibilities of friendship between women of our generation.

The coming together of women in the second-wave women's movement of the late 1960s altered the ways in which they saw themselves. Although it was a sexual liberation movement, a movement committed to giving women proper choices about their bodies, it was as much about the liberation of women into worlds previously denied them. One such area was widening the possibilities for women at work. Working-class women, of course, have always gone to work, out of economic necessity, and some of the jobs that have made women more visible over the past twenty or so years are privileged jobs, for privileged women. But we've learned, too, that all kinds of work, not necessarily only the kind with high status, provides satisfaction for women, and a crucial escape from isolation.

What the women's movement failed to establish in the culture was the importance of motherhood as a job. In fact, because of middle-class women's new preoccupation with work, motherhood may even have lost status in the eyes of the world (i.e. men). (This despite the fact that feminists who have had children sometimes talk as if they invented motherhood.) My mother's occupation, raising children, would have given her no more sense of centrality in the world now than it did a generation ago. Knock hard, life is deaf, as the Surrealists used to say.

It's at the workplace, in the dirty old marketplace, where things have changed. That's where my generation felt we had to make an impact. Work was in some important sense a man's world – a world of sociability, of adventure, of centrality – and we wanted our rights in that world; without it, and the economic independence that went with it, we thought we would always feel marginalized.

Now, in the 1990s, the right to work has become a duty to work for many more women, to service the family debt. Work is by no means a universal panacea: women have never achieved equal pay with men, and employers often use them as cheap labour. It might be tempting, then, to suggest that the virtues of work are overrated. But we still need to remember how much men have ruled the world of work, and through it the world, and how excluded women have felt from it. This is Simone de Beauvoir in 1949:

> The life of the father has a mysterious prestige; the hours he spends at home, the room where he works, the objects he has around him, his pursuits, his hobbies, have a sacred character. He supports the family and he is the responsible head of the family. As a rule his work takes him outside, and so it is through him that the family communicates with the rest of the world: he incarnates that immense, difficult and marvellous world of adventure. (*The Second Sex*)

Since then it has become more accepted that women of all classes work; we are sometimes in charge of money; we sometimes make the large decisions as well as the small; we are not always doing the decorative or supportive jobs. Some would say we got there by making huge compromises with the male-dominated world of work, taking on male values – ambition, efficiency, productivity – or by sacrificing too much else; others think we have sometimes been able to alter and subvert the ways things are done, by doing it our way. Some would say we have tried to have it all – children, work, friends, lovers, husbands – and that it isn't possible. Some think that women who have committed themselves so much to work have made the situation for women who don't work more invidious.

Whatever the arguments, I know that, growing up in the 1950s, I badly needed that sense of belonging out there in the world of work. For various reasons my mother was deprived of it, and I always thought her life would have been easier if she hadn't been. I was afraid of becoming isolated at home, of not belonging, even though my relationship to the world had become much more rooted by becoming a mother. (My longing for children was redeemed by the arrival of my adopted daughter Kate, nine days old, a child I loved so immediately that it felt as if I'd been waiting for her all my life.)

Perhaps very confident women didn't need the kinds of affirmation work gave me. But there are many more like me. True, I eventually had a lovely job, but it was much earlier, being down in the marketplace itself, when I initially acquired that particular sense of being in the real world. And if it is partly a psychological matter, it is certainly also a social one. Work outside the home *counts* in our society. And I think it's this, in the end, that has allowed us to insist that we are still here, that we're not going to go quietly.

It's a slightly grim conclusion. Function is all, ageism reigns supreme. (And of course men may be harder hit than women over this. For many of them, work is too often their total identity. In fact, ageing may be no easier for men – perhaps harder for most.)

There is an additional irony for me in all this. It is exactly in my relationship to work that I have changed most since I began to think of myself as a post-menopausal woman.

What I didn't expect about ageing was how much I would change – psychologically, spiritually, whatever you call it. (A friend told me she felt she'd changed more between fifty and fifty-five than at any time since adolescence.) No doubt some of it is finally feeling a grown-up. But it isn't simply that. I have stopped making those very energetic, slightly obsessive shapes for my life. A certain voraciousness has gone; the drive to be in the thick of things, to be obsessionally perfectionist at work, to be successful, has relaxed. My identity seemed to be so tied up with my work, I feared I might disappear without it. But it doesn't seem to have happened, and it is the deepest relief. There is life after work. I still like it – love it, even – but I am not hooked on it, dependent on it, afraid to be without it. I'm less interested in externals, in performances, mine and others. Life is more comic than I used to think. And I begin to believe in my own death, which has altered what I want from life, though it's too early in the business of being older to know exactly what those things are.

I wonder how my mother felt at the age I am now. She wasn't lucky enough to have, in her generation, the other thing which has altered life after the menopause for mine – a range of female friends who have been talking together now for twenty-five or thirty years about their lives and loves. This is an enormous portfolio of accumulated and shared knowledge. In part it has replaced the family ties that for many of my generation have become so much more complicated (though by no means unimportant). Of course lovers, husbands, children, parents can give friendship, love, support. And of course we are not the first generation of women to have close friends. But female friendship has become almost institutionalized among us, and in a world where family and sexual relationships have vastly altered, and become less stable, those friendships represent a kind of certainty that nothing else can.

'Too much talk,' my daughter used to say in the seventies, when we did indeed do a lot of talking. We've been through a lot together, and women from that generation are now ageing together, and can talk about that too if we want to. It's a wonderful piece of luck. I wish that my mother, and her generation, had had more available to them that staunch and comforting world of friends. I think it shows in our faces.

RITE OF PASSAGE
Elizabeth Buchan

I woke up into the darkness and lay, puzzled as to why. It was four o'clock, high summer, and I was bathed in sweat. Even my brain felt sticky. Outside in the street, someone was returning home drunk, and a police siren echoed in the distance.

I raised my arm and felt the dampness slick down to my wrist. Was this it? I asked myself, depression at the idea settling over me. Was this a hot flush?

The answer was no, just summer heat. Nevertheless, the memory has left a residue of unease and foreboding which requires examination.

It could be the result of giving up smoking – corrugated rolls settling down over the hips, the suggestion of a hanging basket under the upper arms, what J. B. Priestley called the 'mammorial' thigh. Or merely the raised consciousness of a forty-something female that leaps to conclusions on waking hot in the night. My outline informs me that I am no longer a nymph. My age says: change lies ahead, possibly soon.

What is this change? When will it take place? Will it be a physical stepping stone on to a different mental and spiritual road? Or merely a lay-by? Can I expect an alteration in my status, in my perceptions, in my powers?

Probably all of these things, and more. Therein lies its terror – and its challenge.

In one sense, the menopause has become a fashionable talking point in the media. After all, it is a relatively new subject to pick over. A hundred years ago, winnowed by disease and childbirth, not many women reached it. Indeed, until rickets (which deformed the pelvic girdle) and sepsis in childbirth had been ironed out in a significant manner, less than 30 per cent of women – compared to the 90 per cent today – who survived childhood survived to the climacteric. Pre-1900, female mortality for women in their thirties was a staggering 23.3 per cent higher than male. Chronic exhaustion, inadequate diet, anaemia and tuberculosis played a part, but a significant factor in this statistic was childbirth and its consequences – gynaecological damage or death was commonplace. I imagine that many women, if they survived to the menopause, were relieved to leave behind a part of their lives which spelt so much danger.

The age when the menopause took place appears to have varied considerably. According to the nineteenth-century anthropologist Oppenheim, Turkish women lost their menses at thirty. His colleague, Vasiliev, reported that forty-five was the average age for Kirghiz women, and Pilsudsky believed that fifty was the mean for Ainu women in Sakhalin. Now, thanks to improved nutrition, the average female in a developed Western country can expect to reach her late forties before she is plunged into hormonal confusion.

The niggle is not knowing *when*. Next year? In three years' time? Whenever it attacks it will be inconvenient, that's for sure, and I find it strange to consider that I will not be able to consult my body about the menopause as I consulted it about its fertility. Therein lies one of the factors that define this change. The menopause does not come to order – I can't sandwich it in between novels or school holidays, and certainly not between breakfast and tea before the children come home. The menopause is not a McDonald's quickie but a slow-cooking *cassoulet* – and just as much of a mess of beans if it goes wrong. The trouble is, I have become accustomed to being in control. For example, I chose when to have my babies (and how to have them). I chose when not to have them. To have the reins rudely snatched out of my hands – and to accept the situation with grace – must be the first step in coming to terms with what is happening.

In his book *A History of Women's Bodies*, Edward Shorter argues that greater life expectancy, the demystification of the female body by modern medicine, and the growth of the companionate couple in Western society have killed off the female 'culture of solace':

By the 1920s, the classical pattern of women's suffering had ended. The physical problems that have driven women into each other's arms for comfort since time out of mind have been alleviated by modern medicine.

That's dandy. Just when I will require solace.

It is true. Try asking – discreetly, of course – my friends and acquaintances about the menopause, and a peculiar hush falls, broken only by the gabble of very young women who, cushioned by years of future menstruation, are very happy to give their views. The *theory* of menopause, of course. Once, I was one of them, but no longer. Despite the media, a conspiracy of silence exists around this peculiarly female phenomenon; the closer you are to the menopause, the thicker this conspiracy is. I understand. The older you are, the more silent you *wish* to be. There is no culture of solace at this juncture because it is not a subject that engenders confidences. I *know* I will not want to admit that I am being abandoned by my hormones. Compare this to the untidy, friendly gaggles that exchange essential information and back-up over nappies, rusks and airborne Milupa.

Why? Magazines and newspapers fall over themselves to promote – rightly – a new orthodoxy which is light years away from Victorian *pudeur*. We are exhorted to be positive, to be welcoming, even, and to face the changes in our physical composition without shrinking.

To the understudy waiting in the wings, those predicted changes seem pretty terrible, shrinking in body height as a result of osteoporosis being only one of the options dished out – increased fat, facial hair, inelastic skin, hot flushes, sleeplessness and the indignity of organs past their sell-by date are the other ingredients. No doubt there are variants, but I am not going to find out about them. All are designed, expressly, it appears, to shrivel our bodies and our functions and separate us out from the women who still possess a full complement of hormones. The Oh-look, she's flushing . . . Tut-tut, we are a little tetchy today, make allowances for her . . . She is a woman of a certain age . . . syndrome which I have sometimes interpreted in facial expressions.

Terrible, too, are the case histories. One woman wrote of sweating drops into her soup at a smart banquet; another of her depression; another of how she longed to die. Yet another recounts how she was forced through the weary process of finding a new doctor who would treat her extreme symptoms because her regular doctor considered her anguish 'natural' and therefore to be endured. (She should have demanded of this unsympathetic practitioner whether he would treat smallpox or a bad verruca. They are, after all, perfectly natural.)

Pregnancy and childbirth are pretty rotten jokes to play on the female, but I cannot help suspecting that the menopause may be nature's last – and most outrageous – grand belly laugh. There are good reasons, of course: regulating the population and ensuring that the younger, healthier body is the one that reproduces. But I wonder why the shedding of the reproductive role has to be achieved at what seems to be, for some women, so much cost?

Born after the Second World War, I have been granted greater freedoms than previous generations of women: to control my sexuality and fertility and to occupy a niche in the job marketplace. Speaking selfishly, after the slow years of childbearing and caring, I want to get a move on and take advantage of these freedoms. Why not? Besides, I owe it to the women who fought to achieve these gains.

The menopause, it seems, throws us back on our bodies, threatens our comfort and picks cruel contrasts between male and female, the older woman and the younger woman. It sets a seal on the ageing process and feeds a fear that we are shedding our femininity, our sexuality and, therefore, our role. Why do I think that? Look around. Except for a tiny minority, older women in our society do not constitute a powerful franchise, even though they now live longer. They are the butt of jokes – mother-in-law, mutton-dressed-as-lamb – often sneered at, often despised. Some fight back, of course; notable examples are Teresa Gorman, Joan Collins, even Jane Fonda – who, by virtue of the fact that they look wonderful at fifty-plus, are subject to comment, much of it double-edged. Consider the public lashing Teresa Gorman received in the recent court case which thoroughly aired the fact that she took HRT, or the scrutiny to which Joan Collins is subjected. Do we ask Michael Heseltine if he wears a wig? Or if he has had plastic surgery? Do we judge him on the issue of whether he takes supplementary hormones or not?

Women at the other extreme can be sought and found on the Clapham omnibus any day of the week, making do because they have to with bargain-basement clothing and shoes designed to make detours around corns. These women are recognizably not fighting the battle to stay young-looking – maybe through poverty, fatigue or general indifference – and are automatically slotted into a certain category that is not accorded either power or influence, except (one hopes) in the domestic arena.

Where will I strike the balance? Even further along the spectrum? 'When I am an old woman,' wrote Jenny Joseph in her much-quoted poem, 'I shall wear purple with a red hat that doesn't go . . .' Eccentricity may propitiate its exponent and bring a certain kind of freedom, but it does not guarantee an easy passage, and it may be asking too much of my more conventional spirit.

What lies in the aftermath of the menopause? The answer is blunt: biological redundancy. Old age. Death.

No wonder HRT is perceived as a lodestone, attracting users who do not welcome the terminal throes of youth. Nor, apart from the safety-factor problem – and I concede that this is a big 'if' – can I see why the theory of it is so controversial. I see no reason why, if my body has functioned efficiently on a specific cocktail of hormones for its adult years, it is considered outrageous, as some pundits have it, to wish to maintain the status quo. Perhaps male doctors and, by extension, other men fear the female dominatrix: a breed of shiny-complexioned, flexible-boned, *thin* superwomen to which their balding heads and shrinking loins will compare badly. In some respects, their fear is understandable. At the rustle of a pill packet, their companions in life – the *companis* with whom they have broken bread over the decades – are granted chemical leave to linger over the dessert a little longer.

Nevertheless, the menopause has to be faced. Making a virtue of necessity is sensible, even courageous, but rather as I prepared for childbirth, I would like to feel that I will tackle this stage with the same good intentions to carry it off well. To be positive.

A fireman once told me that people behave oddly when they are trapped by a fire. Propelled by terror, they hide under a bed or shut themselves in a cupboard. The forty-something female is prone to similar evasions. The most obvious is the Late Baby Fallacy. The urge to climb back into the Laura Ashley smocks of ten years ago is the urge to make a public declaration that, yes, I am still functioning on all four cylinders.

I should quash it.

There is no denying the joy a late baby can bring, especially to a childless couple, but it cannot be ideal that a ten-year-old has a mother of fifty-five-plus cheering from the touchline. Quite apart from other considerations (the needs of the older child are very important) the energy required to field a toddler is considerable: energy, perhaps, that is no longer there. I regale myself with the dangers of late pregnancy, the logistics of accommodating the results, the dislocated dynamics of the existing family, and how I should consider world population levels.

Nevertheless, signalling that I can still prove my fertility is a seductive and powerful necessity linked, I suspect, with a deep-rooted wish not to acknowledge the death of my youth. Imprinted inside me is a paradigm of myself taken at the best stage: young, glowing, still *hopeful*. In a culture dedicated to reinforcing physical ideals, most of which are nonsensical, it is difficult to yield this model up to a truthful likeness. More than anything, the menopause will instruct me to alter the blueprint; suddenly, buying the short skirt and pasting the side-on shot into the photograph album will assume added significance.

Surely, I ask myself, the sum of my preoccupations and fears cannot only be vanity – a concentration on worldly frivolity of the kind Bunyan showed us so well? Yes and no. If I ignore 'vanity' and concentrate, rather, on the word 'world' which, in Old English, carries the meaning 'being' or 'life of man', I think my reservations sharpen into focus.

After the struggle of fitting into life – the muddle of growing up, the exhaustion and stimulation of childbearing and rearing, the efforts to draw warring bits of myself together – I am finding that my forties are often confident, pleasurable years. It is highly satisfactory to walk along their plateau, looking down at the churned-up terrain below. Being forced up another peak *quite* so soon seems unfair.

To some extent, people can be pigeonholed into early and late blossomers. The early ones are those who tuck their adolescence and twenties under their belt. The ones who dominate school groups and look good in leggings – or the fashion equivalent – from the word go. They are at ease, and tend to have a physical appearance that fits the vogue. They wax strong on the exhilaration and seesaw of youth. They manage being young well.

The late blossomers, like me, look on. Uneasy. Fretful, sometimes lumpen, often unhappy. What is the ingredient, they ask themselves, that they lack?

Then time performs one of its tricks. The late blossomer does just that. Blossoms. I found purpose, peace, a degree of contentment, the right job, a role in being a parent. Longings coalesced, mistakes were tackled. Satisfaction grows, and a knowledge that life can be accommodated multiplies my sense of achievement. At last, there is a measure of control.

Aha.

The menopause is *caesura*, a formal stop to fertility, which I cannot prevent. Move over, it will tell me. Make room. Its capaciousness, its ingratitude, the emotional luggage it drags with it, the autumn landscape the other side, fill me with gloom.

Are there no compensations?

As I will no longer be the bleeding, mysterious creature so mistrusted throughout the ages ('Nothing is so unclean as a woman in her periods, what she touches she causes to become unclean,' wrote St Jerome, apparently terrified by the fertile woman's capacity to pollute), can I expect to be treated equally from now on?

The curse of Eve removed, the pacifically female function shed, Nature is presumably at liberty to treat both sexes equally. Male and female can both die of heart disease, cancer, and the rest in perfect equality. Not a bit of it. The privilege of fertility is extended to the male until the day he dies, and how many males end up with splintered bones and a dowager's hump?

Can I expect greater rewards in the public workplace? After all, whether I like it or not, I have more experience than those younger than me. Not necessarily. Ageism is rampant, and there are younger, better-looking women coming up fast who are not proffering solace, only competition. I may not like it, nor is it laudable, but to be attractive in our society is a source of power, exploited daily everywhere. Stern feminists and those who do not benefit – or have chosen not to – from this advantage might howl at this last statement. They would be right, but I think I must be honest: it is *true* whether it is a good state of affairs or not, whether it is fashionable to acknowledge it or not, and – being, as my son says, 'passable' – I have deployed that power . . . from time to time. Of course you can argue that age will remove that option, and so it will. Nevertheless, the menopause underlines the transition from a state where sexuality, both conscious and unconscious, is a base ingredient to a different state where it will be necessary to relearn the rules.

Will I, dare I, seek release from the tyranny of the beauty straitjacket: from a calorie-dominated existence where cellulite is a certifiable disease? I hope I will be strong enough to abandon its more tedious aspects. If you agree that many women, from the first pink Baby-gro, are netted by fear and inadequacy into a conspiracy to make us look as we think men wish us to look, then to give it up is, perhaps, progress. For the first time, I might dig into the bran tub of my own inclinations, abandon a regime of Flora and skimmed milk, and embark on chocolate binges. To wake up each morning liberated from the bondage of wishing myself a stereotype, free to jump into a shapeless skirt and to wear eccentric jumpers. Free to become 42-plus round the hips, to abandon shiny Lycra tights and to give up on ordeal-by-workout.

Hang on. Joan Collins, Jane Fonda, Raquel Welch may be asked impertinent questions about their age and whether they indulge in face-lifts and body-sculpting (and I admit to being fascinated by the details), but by virtue of this very fact they are being offered to us as icons. On what basis are we invited to admire and to emulate? This sort of woman has chosen *not* to avail herself of the above freedoms, and travelled in a contrary direction to those women on the Clapham omnibus. Look at us, their lip-glossed lips invite, look at our teeny-weeny hips and our smoothly landscaped faces. Look at our youthfulness. We have beaten Nature. It was tough, expensive and painful, but take heart – we have done it, and you should, too, if you want to enjoy our sort of status. Why? I am forced to conclude that their heroic efforts in the quest for eternal youth are the reflection of a culture terrorized by the idea that we die. By pushing back the frontiers of ageing, they are perceived to be vanquishing death.

This palpable fallacy is no comfort at all to me. Emphatically I do not want to die, but die I must, wrinkled or not. If the world acknowledges pretty ladies, not saggers in tweed skirts; if I have failed to reach film-star salary or chosen to give it to the local hospice rather than spend it on my body; if I do not have much time to spare on personal appearance, nor do I think it right to spend a large proportion of my time and money in a world so beset by serious problems, the essentially narcissistic icon offered by Collinses, Fondas and Welches is a limited – and limiting – blueprint for post-menopausal survival. This leaves me to mourn the loss of my younger self and to weather a tricky relationship with the orange-peel thigh, the – oh my God – spreading crow's feet and the grey hair that can no longer be explained away as an attractive freak of Nature.

Ah well, in all cultures there must be space for the wiser, older woman who does not look like a film star, as there is, increasingly, for the second-hand car and recycled paper in ours. If we don't make sure there is, the growing band, the new icon-makers, must.

So here I am. Mothering, writing, working, coping. Life is an exercise in critical path analysis, but somehow my children and my work dovetail: sometimes awkwardly, sometimes by sailing dangerously close to the wind. Sometimes the ship runs aground, but floats off again on the following tide. It is an outward existence: nurturing, organizing, directing – an exemplar, let it be said, of feminine power; and there is richness, sustenance and pleasure in plenty to be had.

Bang.

The menopause signals an attack. On my body. On my

mental equilibrium. A 360-degree turnabout which may render me as unsettled as my teenage children. What rotten timing.

If I survive, layers will be shed from now on. My children will cut themselves off from the main trunk; my nurturing role must, of necessity, etiolate. My work will shrink and, in one sense, my power will diminish.

But just as the discomforts of pregnancy and the pain of childbirth were followed by the life-giving and precious rewards of being a parent, so, perhaps, will the aridity of the menopause yield to a more fertile landscape. It will be time to face inward.

The Hindu practice of *sadhu* provides a neat parallel. When the children are settled into families of their own, the parents can choose to shed their worldly possessions, don a white robe for renunciation and set off on a pilgrimage which, if it surely leads to death, goes via spiritual enlightenment. No longer earthed by a taproot, no longer embroiled in the (often bruising) business of rearing children and keeping afloat in family politics, the *sadhu* sets you free. You may, if you allow yourself the time and commitment, 'become what you are'. As a German philosopher wrote, there is now space for God to come 'to birth in the soul'.

I look forward (yes, I know, a bit late) to a prolonged lick and polish of my Self: the Self I do not always like, and wish fervently was not prone to fits of martyrdom, inferiority, grumbling, panic and gloom. Nevertheless, I cannot send it back with an offended note from the unsatisfied consumer – I learned that in my twenties and thirties – but I can submit it for a refit. This I shall do, knowing that only by absorbing the bits of me that are lonely, vulnerable and unacceptable, the grim side, can I reach wholeness. After all, my temper makes me me and, providing it is not unleashed as a bad habit, there is no sense in denying it.

Neither is it useful to say: I shall never grumble. Some things *need* grumbling about. I hope, too, that I shall be ready to listen to others, be prepared to ask for help if I need it, be there as a trusted presence for my family and friends, ignore rules and not flee from the spectacle of pain in others because it makes me aware of my own. Perhaps, too, I will be able to look back and, with the help of the spring-cleaned Self, extract sense from any waste and muddle in the past.

In this way, the menopause is deeply useful: a time to consider the spiritual life, the health of my Self, and to initiate the process of withdrawal from my children. As a female, I am granted this reminder to do so in good time.

As my bones leech of their calcium and turn brittle so, too, will my body wither, leaving my mind to expand along other paths. I am free to take on what, I imagine, will be an exhilarating – if demanding – struggle towards comprehension.

No leave-taking is without pain. I will grieve for the years of the flesh, of the now, of being wanted and sucked dry by others, of being young, sweet-fleshed and acceptable. To say goodbye to the knowledge that life lies behind, not ahead, is hard and bitter. So, too, is the fear of the unknown. Where next? Where am I placed?

There will be time to contemplate my place in the cosmos, and to come to terms with the helplessness this can engender. To fence with the idea of our random universe, to tussle for a sense of proportion in the presence of vast questions, to tolerate uncertainty with better equanimity.

Will I be able to gaze unblinking at the prospect of the end? To decide that death is a finale, or a door through which I will emerge into something else?

Who knows?

DRUNKEN DROWNING
Sheila MacLeod

Being a literal-minded sort of person, I had always envisaged the menopause as an event: something finite and final; firmly rooted in time and instantly recognizable. This notion represented the triumph of language over experience. I knew very well that adolescence was less an event to be recognized by the start of menstruation than a long and often painful process involving a whole series of gradual readjustments. Yet I persisted in believing in some corner of my mind, which I preferred not to visit too often, that the whole process could be repeated in reverse at a stroke, and the state of prime adult womanhood would come to a full stop.

It seems to me now that on some level which emerged only intermittently into consciousness, I equated the menopause with death. It was something in the very far distant future, something which happened to other people, but not to me – not yet. And it was certainly something which could not be contemplated for long without a sense of horror.

There was another factor, not usually prominent in discussions of death (although perhaps it should be): embarrassment. We tend to respect death, according it some dignity, and if our voices are hushed when we pronounce the word, we don't exchange furtive glances or snigger at it behind our hands. But I saw the menopause (inasmuch as I saw it at all) as a source of shame and indignity: definitely something to keep quiet about if and when the dire moment struck. Once again, as in adolescence, the treacherous body would assume control, proclaiming itself erroneously as the true self, the totality of what I was.

Given the information generally available over the last few decades, my fears and attempts at evasive action are understandable, if not entirely justifiable. The menopause may not be the equivalent of death, but it is inextricably part of the ageing process and as such, until very recently, a taboo subject for open public discussion. The affluence of the so-called developed world has given us the twin illusions of progress and immortality – illusions which we are unwilling to relinquish. In such a climate, youth (with its connotations of sexual and reproductive activity) equals Good; so age (with its contrary connotations) must equal Bad. However deluded it may be, such has been the prevailing morality for most of my adult life.

The cult of youth has always been a particularly insidious one for women because we are identified (whether we like it or not) with our bodies and reproductive function in ways which men have been spared. The post-menopausal woman has long been the butt of popular ridicule, of which the mother-in-law joke is only the most notorious example. In D. H. Lawrence's novel *The Plumed Serpent* the fortyish heroine, Kate Leslie, decides to stay in Mexico as a member of a macho cult she cannot take seriously rather than return to London and join the ranks of 'the grimalkins in the drawing-rooms of Europe'. The epithet is so precise: a sleekly submissive domestic pet has acquired the independence and rapacity of its wild ancestors. Lawrence's work is full of diatribes against the terrible longevity of the desexed older woman who has outlived her usefulness.

Lawrence's attitude is not, of course, unique to him, and his prejudices are those which many a woman of around my age must have absorbed on some level or other of consciousness. Something terrible happens to women at around the age of fifty, something superadded to the process of ageing, which turns them into monsters. It is this: they are no longer women (in the sense of being desirable partners for men), yet they persist in behaving as if they were. This behaviour is risible, grotesque, pathetic – and dangerous, particularly to men.

The other, obverse myth of the post-menopausal woman was that of someone who had accepted her loss of femininity. 'Gracefully' was the adverb most generally used to describe this process, and it was usually breathed with a sigh of relief: so the old girl wasn't going to cause any trouble after all. The 'good' post-menopausal woman's duty was to become invisible. Readers of Doris Lessing will be familiar with the scene in *The Summer Before the Dark* where the heroine, another Kate, walks down the same street twice: once sporting all the finery and signs of youth that money can buy; once in an old coat and headscarf, with no make-up. The first time she attracts all sorts of comments and whistles from a gang of building workers. The second time, she does not merit even a glance. She can be ignored; she does not exist.

With such myths so firmly and deeply embedded that they were incapable of acknowledgement, it is small wonder that I was not exactly looking forward to 'going through The Change', and preferred to adopt the ostrich position. My own mother died at around the time of the menopause (mid-fifties) and had been ill for some time before that, so there were no familial examples from which I might have taken heart. Had she been alive as I neared my forties, we might then have talked about ageing and all it entails. As it was, I don't think I ever talked to anyone – apart from ruefully comparing wrinkles and grey hairs. And if anyone talked to me, I'm sure I didn't listen.

My attitude towards my body has typically been: I don't want to know. It has almost always been something not to be trusted, an enemy which may be pacified from time to time but never entirely appeased. I have a generally fatalistic attitude towards illness, never go for check-ups, and tend to assume that the organism will break down and fall apart one day anyway, just like a car. And just as with my car, although there are moments when we are in perfect accord, most of the time I am cursing it for failing inexplicably to do what it should, what I want it to.

So when, at the age of forty-four, I was forced to admit that I didn't seem to have had a period for at least three months, I assumed (with mixed feelings) that I was pregnant. So did my GP and, by a fluke, an inaccurate test confirmed our suppositions. I was totally unprepared to discover, a week or so later, that my symptoms must be menopausal.

For whatever reason (late menarche; a history of anorexia; prolonged use of the contraceptive pill), I was going through the menopause comparatively early. Once I had recovered from the initial shock, my reaction was: so what? All it meant was no more bleeding every month; and good riddance too. I looked the same, I felt the same, and people responded to me in the same way as before. If this was the menopause, it was a cinch. What was all the fuss about?

But, inevitably, that was not the whole story, and from

that moment of happy-go-lucky triumph I began to enter a different, often nightmarish, emotional world. Of course we all change all the time throughout our lives, but the process is usually so gradual as to be almost imperceptible, especially to ourselves. The extraordinary aspect of this phase of my life was that I was fully aware of a whole internal drama being played out, over which I seemed to have no control. I concluded that the menopause was, alternately, like drowning and like being drunk.

For the first time I felt I really understood the line 'All time is eternally present'. It was not exactly that my whole life flashed before my eyes, but I certainly saw it all as if on a wide, wide screen because it had come to stay, demanding house room until I gave it the necessary attention. Places or people I had 'forgotten' would suddenly come to mind for no apparent reason, and with all the clarity they possessed at the time. I loved them, hated them, admired them, despised them, just as I had then. Similarly 'forgotten' incidents would replay themselves with a change of emphasis or an added significance which had previously eluded me.

Everything seemed to be connected to something else, to be something beyond itself, and life became a series of Proustian sensations. My madeleines were old pop songs, a phrase in Gaelic, a whiff of school dinners, even the voice of a child in the supermarket calling 'Mum!' on just the right insistent note. A photograph, a discarded garment, a change in the weather, all served the same purpose. The list would be endless. Anything heard or glimpsed accidentally might well trigger the process of recall. 'I'd always thought of being old as terribly boring,' a friend of a similar age remarked (somewhat prematurely, in my opinion), 'but my inner life is so crowded I hardly have time to sleep.' I knew what she meant.

Much of this quasi-drowning process was pleasant – if

always imbued with nostalgia and a kind of disbelief that so much should so suddenly have become history. But much of it was painful, too, as if all the old wounds had conspired to reopen together. And – to continue the Proustian theme – it was Shakespeare's sonnet about remembrance of things past which often seemed to sum up my emotional state. I too was prone to 'grieve at grievances foregone' and to

> drown an eye unused to flow
> For precious friends hid in death's dateless night,
> And weep afresh love's long since cancell'd woe
> And moan the expense of many a vanish'd sight.

All time may have been eternally present, but it was simultaneously and paradoxically part of the receding and all-too-impermanent past.

Only gradually did I discover that other women were going through similar experiences – some becoming enraged, some bitter, some defiant, some resigned. This was when I began to see the menopausal process as akin to that of being drunk, in that alcohol too depresses the inhibitors which keep us acting with the required social decorum. (And, for all I know, a similar chemical process may be involved.) While I would not altogether subscribe to the theory *in vino veritas*, I have noticed that alcohol tends to make nice people nicer and nasty people nastier. Or, to put it less judgementally, it exposes the ruling passion of the drinker, a passion which he/she is then likely to put into action.

My own ruling passion soon resolved itself into a sense of loss. I was 'really' (I was convinced at the time) a griever, a mourner. And I began to be haunted by ancestral images of black-clad women keening on the Hebridean shore for the boats and the men who would never come back. When a long-lost (actually, never-met) relative from my native

Isle of Lewis contacted me, I was eager to enter into correspondence. She knew more about the MacLeods (my father and my mother were both MacLeods) than I did, and I soon became fascinated by tales of misspent talent, crises of conscience, rifts within the Church and examples of extraordinary stoicism. I began to wonder why I had never bothered to investigate family history before. The concepts of roots and blood-relation took on a new, sometimes urgent, importance.

It seemed that identity was once again an issue, as it had been in adolescence. Only this time there was more of it to grapple with: more limitations to be recognized, and at the same time more room for regret. Whenever I heard Edith Piaf singing *Je ne regrette rien* (all too often, it seemed) I wanted to throw something at her. Only the blandest of idiots could possibly have no regrets. I regretted everything, even ever having been born. But there was an oddly liberating comfort to be gained from this extremity.

It is difficult to know how much of my emotional turmoil was attributable to something called the menopause, and how much simply (or not so simply) to the process of getting older. Common sense tells us that sooner or later we need to confront and come to terms with the causes for grief, anger, bitterness, whatever, which have been troubling us and which we have pushed aside. It is not surprising that middle age should be a time for dealing with unfinished business. But when the process is speeded up and intensified, common sense leads us in turn to suppose that chemical changes in the body are at least partially responsible.

All the most recent research into the effects of the menopause seems to be coming to the conclusion that hormonal changes in themselves contribute little to a woman's subjective perception of the process. States of anxiety and depression are not the direct results of bioendocrine changes but, rather, are linked to the outward circumstances of a woman's life on which her integrity and self-esteem depend. Such conclusions would be too obvious to need stating, were it not for the myths surrounding the menopausal woman as someone driven to crazy, irrational behaviour by mysterious and sadly inevitable biological upsets.

The psychosocial factors which affect a woman's functioning in the menopausal years are variously listed as the empty nest syndrome, poor familial or sexual relationships, the illness or death of parents, poor physical health, growing old in a youth-centred culture, and 'negative' expectations or attitudes. Feminism emerges as a good influence, femininity (in the traditional sense) as a handicap. One study, which I found particularly relevant, indicates that timing is all-important, and that women who experience the menopause as and when expected have fewer problems than do those of us who go through it either very early or very late.

It seems to be assumed in the academic literature that a 'good' menopause is one you take in your stride, sail through, or hardly notice. I am reminded of the commendation often bestowed on babies by women of my mother's generation: 'You'd never know he/she was in the house.' Even as a child I found this odd, feeling that if I ever had a baby, that was precisely what I would want to know; otherwise, why bother? And I doubt if anxiety, depression and anguish can be ignored with impunity any more than babies can. Pain is only a symptom, after all; its purpose is to alert us to its own underlying cause.

Sometimes a tone of moral stricture creeps into these otherwise worthy treatises. The menopausal woman who has no problems (i.e. behaves as if nothing untoward were happening to her) is hailed as a well-adjusted citizen; whereas those who articulate or act out their distress are deemed to be inadequate copers with low self-esteem. The implication, as so often elsewhere, is that self-control is the prime feminine virtue. With all due respect to the ameliorative intentions of such research, I submit that this is a load of codswallop. The copers are not better people than the rest of us. They're just luckier. Or perhaps less honest.

Because most of the research I have come across is American, it is hardly surprising that neo-positivistic attitudes should predominate. But the popular literature on the subject, which is also US-led, seems hellbent on making Pollyannas of us all, and has me, at least, craving a shot of good old European angst. I resent and resist the evangelists who tell me all the news is good, reassuring me, amid exhortations to keep smiling through, that drugs and/or cosmetic surgery will make me feel happy, sexy and young. (The three are synonymous in the vocabulary of this particular gospel.) But suppose I want to be happy some other way? Suppose I am perverse enough to suspect that getting old might actually be an interesting and important experience?

The drug companies have clearly done a splendid promotional job on hormone replacement therapy, because I never hear or read a word against it. It is a panacea. It will make us all young and beautiful for ever – and never mind the side-effects. For every uncomfortable or painful symptom (including states of mind) there is an appropriate drug. We can have bits cut off us, and other bits (or even the same ones) added on elsewhere. Oh wow, have we got age by the throat! Have we got death at bay! All that's needed is a cheerful, optimistic attitude and loadsamoney.

Whenever I hear this whistling in the dark I am ironically reminded of myself at my most profoundly anorexic, when I believed that in starving myself into amenorrhoea I had made time run backwards by an effort of my own will. Eminent professors of psychiatry have labelled this sort of anorexic thinking psychotic. It is not a word I would use, but it is surely a form of mass delusion to imagine that in pretending to be young we can conquer time and, by extension, death itself. Wish-fulfilment is for dreams. In waking life it is a hindrance, and eventually becomes a bore: sword and sorcery for senior citizens.

The pressure is on us all to deny reality. And if we are women, the pressure is directed with particular weight towards the denial of anything in our experience which could be called 'negative'. Male struggles and agonies are the stuff of literature, but a woman who attempts to describe those of her own sex is likely to be castigated as self-indulgent and told that she has not distanced herself sufficiently from her subject matter. Our struggles and agonies are not to be taken seriously because our lives are of peripheral rather than central concern. So chin up, ladies, take another pill and, bless you, you'll feel ever so much better! The subtext of which is: we (younger women as well as men) will feel ever so much better if you reassure us that ageing is painless instead of confronting us with a daily *memento mori*.

While I understand the temptation to go along with the lie, I prefer to claim the right to my own pain, the right to its expression. I value my dark night of the menopausal soul. I cherish it because it was necessary for my future well-being, and without it I should have missed an enlightening and enriching experience. Admittedly, the belief that growth can come out of suffering, out of meeting rather than denying experience, is too deeply ingrained in my Scottish Presbyterian soul for me to feel otherwise. But now that the turmoil has abated, I know that I have come through a rite of passage and (inasmuch as I am capable of any such sentiment) gained a sense of achievement.

It is not that I am of the alternative school of thought which urges us to embrace our haghood with open arms. I am as averse as the next woman to becoming wrinkled, hairy and decrepit. Objectively speaking, there is little to be said in favour of old age – scarcely more, really, than there is to be said in favour of dying, and sometimes considerably less. But to refuse to advocate it is not the same as denying that it happens, and must happen. What remains is to glean from it what we can and may.

And there are a few perks if you happen to be solvent and in reasonably good health. When I was a child I often looked forward to being old because then (as I saw it) I would be freed from the necessity of having to prove myself; by then I would know who and what I was. In my adolescence the chief virtue of age seemed to be a freedom from the obligation to be sexually attractive and the burden of having to deal with the consequences. As a young woman I could see age as a period when it was possible to be as selfish, bad-tempered and autocratic as you pleased; and no one would dare to contradict you. All those suppositions are proving at least partially true. They add up to a liberation from the shifts of the false self who must please and appease in order to be rewarded, to be validated and loved.

Some of my youthful fears about ageing and the menopause are also proving partially true, but in an odd, backhanded sort of way. 'I wouldn't start from here if I were you,' says the joke Irishman (I've always considered him eminently sensible) on being asked the way to Dublin. Just as a hill which looks dauntingly steep in the distance flattens out when we approach it, so some of the attributes of ageing which are horrifying from the perspective of youth turn out to be both appropriate and acceptable to middle age: quite bearable, after all, and sometimes even welcome. Subjective experience belies objective assessment, and one man's grimalkin is another woman's indomitable survivor.

I see my menopausal years as a time for clearing out

unwanted lumber and sorting out priorities: a time of crystallization. It is not that I am any more certain about anything, but I am inclined to allow myself – and, by extension, the world – to contain contradictions. Indeed, life seems more than ever a matter of chance and paradox rather than a series of problems to be solved or overcome. And I am left wondering how appropriate it is to regard any one of its stages as inherently more problematic than another.

Irreparable physical damage aside, being fifty or sixty is surely no more of a 'problem' than being ten, twenty, thirty or forty. However old you are, you're mortal. Isn't that exactly what makes life as interesting, precious, cruel, unjust and altogether extraordinary as it is?

David Sillitoe

And Then There Was One

Penelope Farmer

The crush bar at Covent Garden during the long interval of one of Wagner's Ring Cycle operas might induce the odd hot flush at any age; it is not otherwise the most likely place for reflections on the menopause. But there I was – at *Götterdämmerung*, I think, appropriately enough – in an interminable queue for alcohol or coffee, and the unmistakable voice proclaimed just behind me: 'Let the strength of the menopause come to our rescue . . .' It could only be – it was – Germaine Greer herself, wrestling with a wine bottle, a corkscrew, a recalcitrant cork. So, Germaine, I love you; how could I not? Precisely of my age and generation, you – with a few others – defined the stereotypes, named them, throughout the physical and emotional rites of passage: at adolescence, marriage, motherhood; divorce. And now, in our early fifties, at this: the dreaded, whispered-about, what-we-all-have-to-put-up-with-dear (they said the same thing about menstruation and labour pains) – the menopause.

Only last night, on the 'Late Show', you read out loud the passage in your book which delineates the fatal image – the one your friend, in your version, could not bear to contemplate: the little old woman in grey trotting along with her *baguette*, invisible to the world. You, on the other hand, appeared in some sense to accept such an image – indeed, as good as recommended it to the rest of us. In some ways, of course, you are right to. There is nothing wrong with either being or looking like a little old woman – who but the old woman herself knows what goes on in any such female head; has no one else noticed how the more demure the 'little' 'grey' person, the more male and randy the little dog that accompanies it? There was an ex-ballet dancer in our street once – very trim, neat, behatted, all of eighty at a guess. She had a cairn terrier called Hamish that hared after every bitch in sight, watched, benevolently, by its mistress.

But there are other images, Germaine. I can't seriously see you, for one, scurrying along with your *baguette*. Nor is it unreasonable to dread the disintegrations of old age, and to defer them by any means offered. This is nothing to do with not accepting the inevitable, let alone with wanting to perpetuate sex-kittenhood; not all those who take HRT do so because they aspire to Joan Collins; it is just a whole lot better than osteoporosis. And who says we need stop being, appearing, sexy, even minus Joan Collins for a role-model? Martha Gellhorn is still sexy aged eighty – Peggy Ashcroft was – Naomi Mitchison was, aged ninety or so, when I last saw her, on television. Outside stereotype, Page Three, the newsagent's top shelf, it's not a factor of age – just of how you are on the one hand, how you look at it on the other. And of what you mean by the word 'sexy'.

The difference, of course, is a matter of choice; it is

easier to take it now or leave it. And what loss there is – must be – in the loss of libido, fertility, and the rest of it, is more than made up for by that partial, not wholly illusionary, freedom. Some things have to be accepted; the sex game must change in certain respects – aspects of playing the sexual field I can't help sighing for, they were such *fun*. But then I mourned aspects of childhood at adolescence, aspects of single life at marriage, aspects of childlessness at motherhood; we lose – and gain – from beginning to end, and all the way back again. There's nothing odd in it, let alone tragical.

And for me, it's all somewhat academic anyway. All things being equal, I might prefer to be Martha Gellhorn or Peggy Ashcroft, rather than a woman in grey with a *baguette*, yet when it comes to it, I don't mind what I am like when I'm sixty, seventy, eighty, I just want to be there if possible, and still in my right mind. I'd rather be a little old lady with my *baguette*, with or without my randy little dog, any day; I'd rather be a little old man, Germaine, than irrevocably dead at fifty.

For no matter how much we attempt to talk for women in general, all of us have our own agendas on this matter. Mine don't – I hope – mean that I reject the reality of the other issues; up to a point I still *feel* them, think they're worth discussing. But please understand why, in regard to this rite of passage, my main agenda is somewhat different. I come from a family with a dominant defective gene. My mother died, aged fifty-three, of breast cancer; my twin sister died last year, aged fifty-one, of the same disease. Her grandchildren will not know her – any more than her children knew their grandmother, or we knew ours for that matter, or my mother hers; to my certain knowledge that's four grandmotherless generations; farther back I don't know, I can't follow. As for me – well, here I still am, give or take a few wild moods, a few hot flushes – give or take a minor brush with my sister's, my mother's, dread lurgy, ten years back. If here I still am in five – or, better still, ten – years; if I can see my grandchildren, watch them grow up, write a few more books, go to a few more places, live, that's enough for me. What's it matter, the loss of the odd hormone?

Losing my mother, my sister, when I did was something else; even more than my fear of going that way myself. For me, if menopause means anything it means that loss; it means not pause, in that sense, but stop. And why 'pause', by the way, in general – why not 'stop'? There's a real danger in that wistful word – pause implies a temporary stop, a hope of resumption, rather than an acceptance of change. I remember the woman in Thomas Mann's weird – not to say perverse, not to say horrible – *Black Swan*. (How ironic that the first – still one of the only – novels about the menopause, if you discount Margaret Drabble's latest, was written by a man; the fact that it was written by a man presumably explains its ironies, not to say its almost pathological pathos.) A post-menopausal woman falls in love, and then discovers that she is bleeding again and hopes, hopes; only to discover that what she is welcoming is not fertility but death: cancer. As with my sister. Stop. Not just 'no more bleeding'; no more body to bleed with. That's the image which haunts me – how could it not? As indeed it defines my particular, menopausal – meno*stop*al – task; I resist, you will notice, the word 'problem'.

I suppose that at this point I could sit down to write a piece about 'How I Came to Terms with My Own Mortality'. But no, I don't propose to. Of course, in the circumstances, I've had to try to come to terms with such things. But then, who does not? The point about the menopause is, precisely, that in the course of it women in general confront their own mortality; must, in the light of it, redefine their sense of themselves somewhat or go under.

On that reckoning, what I've had to face in my sister's body – in mine too, for that matter – is a more extreme, more clear-cut version of the matter: no more, no less; all of us around the age of fifty watch our parents, most probably, and certainly their generation, disintegrate, start dying; all of us catch the ominous warnings of such disintegration in our own bodies.

I'm not saying that even for me this isn't important, that I don't reflect on it, that I don't get the odd fright from the odd unexplained physical twinge; of course I do. But the fact is that for me, now, it feels as if I've been through all that, and out the other side. It feels nothing, nothing, compared to the matter of working through the loss of my sister, through the whole psychic business of being one of a pair since birth, and now no longer; compared to the guilt of being the one for whom, gloriously – in spite of the loss, in spite of a survivor's guilt – middle age doesn't physically mean pause in any fatal sense, doesn't mean stop – yet; just continuation. This means that I am able to sit upstairs in the room where I work, as I do now, looking out at our local chapter of swifts diving and screaming; sniffing summer and paper and computer smells and my own lively flesh; reflecting on the fact that the flesh of my sister, with whom I shared a womb, is scented no more; is no more; is earth, dust, ashes, in a churchyard in Oxfordshire; that she is what I will be – what, oddly enough, I don't fear being – eventually: a skeleton on the one hand, a memory on the other. Better to think about it than not, I assure you. These days I welcome those seventeenth-century portraits, seventeenth-century tombs, which scarcely discriminate between skulls and cherubs, ends and beginnings. Is not all life like mine now, a matter of ends and beginnings? But please God, not my end yet, not for ten years at least – or longer. Let the search, the investigation, continue, in the process of which I find myself discovering not just what I am, but what she was also. There is no other way I can let go of her, being part of her, along with the rest.

At the age of eighteen, was it, or twenty? – I don't remember – my twin and I looked at the life our mother led, and then at each other, and said, out loud – mostly we did not communicate such things out loud – 'This is not going to happen to us.' And maybe it didn't. Or maybe it did. We certainly, neither of us, led lives like our mother's. My sister died very angry, just the same; and I do not think that she was angry with death only. She had a very good reason for being angry with me, after all, even though she would have acknowledged – she always was fair about such things – that I couldn't be blamed for my survival. She left me her anger, along with her two more or less grown-up children. One of my menopausal tasks – like the women in the fairy tales counting hay seeds, spinning straw – is keeping my distance from that; is describing, understanding it; is not, for heaven's sake, taking it on, absorbing it, the way over the years I absorbed, as she did, our likeness and unlikeness. To keep absorbing her like that would be to wish myself into her death, in some way. As it is hard enough not to.

Being twins – not identical twins, but sufficiently alike for people to enjoy fitting us to the charming stereotype: What delightful bridesmaids we were! Oh, how in demand for the weddings of strangers! – we were perfectly accustomed to people saying, 'Your twin is wearing red today, why aren't you?' 'Your twin got 10 out of 10 for maths, why didn't you?' 'Your twin is in the school play, why aren't you?'; it would have seemed strange if they hadn't done so. For of course we internalized such questions; they came very early to be part of what we felt ourselves to be – so much so that my sister wrote 'From one half to the other' in the book about Paolo Uccello she gave me for our twenty-first birthday. So much so that still, thinking of her grave, I can almost hear the whisper, 'If your twin is dead already, why aren't you?' And do not know how to reject such a whisper outright, even as on another level I rejoice in being alive; and so, by definition, rejoice in our *de facto* separation.

I was not in England when she was diagnosed, had her mastectomy. My first response on hearing about it was not fear or grief, but sheer rage that she should have let them mutilate her in such a way – I had not let them do it to me. I suspect that even after all these years, I saw her body as in some sense mine; mine, too, the mutilation. Of course I did not tell her I was angry, though I agonized later, seeing the painful after-effects – a swollen arm, and so forth – about which, of course, no one had warned her. (I could have warned her, but by the time I came on the scene it was all too late.) The recurrence, new tumours, appeared six months later; so many, so suddenly, it did not look good. I went away then, and sat by myself in a cottage in Derbyshire, working through fear and grief, and guilt that it was her, not me; and relief, I had to admit, that it was her, not me. It was at this stage, contemplating the all-too-real possibility of her death, that I first had the image which was to haunt me until long after her funeral: the image of her open grave as a black rectangle into which I too was irrevocably drawn, into which I envisioned myself jumping, unable to help myself, as if sharing a womb with her meant it was my duty also, my fate, to share her grave. Her anger, I felt, was because I, despite everything, showed no signs of doing so; my anger because, in the face of such reality, rage was easier than fear and guilt. Seeing another good night better not to go gentle into, I raged, raged, against her anger as against the dying of her light.

The rage – hers and mine – had always been there, though, from the beginning. We fought not to be separated;

but put together we fought each other – so fiercely that when we were very small our toys had to be soft toys which, bashed over the other's head, could do no damage. Once, I remember, when we were older – six or so – the object in contention between us was a pair of cutting-out scissors. In the course of the battle for it, she cut me – barely, but enough to draw blood from my little finger. Whereupon she ran away and hid for four hours at the bottom of the garden, and could not be found. I don't remember the incident – or I didn't; but she never forgot it. When I was reminded of it after her death by someone to whom she'd recounted the story, all that came back to me was the fine thread of blood upon my finger; also this image of the dark, curled-up figure of my guilty sister among the rhododendron bushes. Not that I ever saw her there; I just imagine that was how it was. Apart from which – this I'd forgotten also but she, once again, had not – there'd been the day they told us of the death of our week-old brother. She hadn't wanted to see him; she thought he died because of that. She fed on the guilt of it; but where did such guilt come from? – it wasn't like anything I felt. Whereas she spent the rest of her life expiating it in one way and another – as social worker, probation officer, and so on. Seething with rage. Giving herself, the self-styled criminal, no quarter. Giving me no quarter, come to that.

I don't know what image she had of me – mine of her can be summed up by a photograph left over from my second wedding. My husband and I are kissing each other; the registrar has just pronounced us man and wife. And there in the background, among the other members of our families, sits my sister, frowning, looking on, the light reflected on her glasses hiding an expression I do not need to see, can read perfectly well from what she's wearing, from the way she sits, from the fixed horizontal of her mouth. She was acting out not only what she was, what she felt towards me, but what I projected on to her – it goes without saying. I could not see or hear her without a *frisson* of some kind all those later years – a *frisson* I still feel, looking at that picture. There she sits, the image of my conscience, my superego, the source of *my* rage, frustration, bodily identity, resentment. As I, no doubt, made such an image, such a source, for her – not least on that occasion. Too much hangs on an act as profound as marriage for it ever to be neutral, within families; between us – for her, particularly, who at the times of both my marriages was not herself attached – it had the force of a statement of belief, religious, political, philosophical; dangerous stuff. I wanted her to rejoice for me. I found it hard to forgive her then because she so plainly could not. Now I have to forgive her; seeing that picture makes me want to weep. Here was a woman in whom the world brought out the best – two hundred people with whom she had worked as probation officer, as drug counsellor, came to her memorial service; and all I ever did was bring out the worst in her, it often seemed; as she, also all too often, brought out the worst in me.

The thing about being a twin, what draws you together as co-conspirators, is the insidiously beguiling fact that the world not only sees you that way; that it also – envious, perhaps, of the union with another, the kind everyone is supposed to long for from the moment of separation from the mother – seems to want you to be co-conspirators. Just like women, twins are, in that way, victims of the image other people have of them – an image largely related, as with women again, to what other people need them to be, rather than what they actually are as their separate selves. As women we have the chance, the necessity, to redefine ourselves around the age of fifty. For twins, even growing up, embarking on separate careers, doesn't provide any such opportunity, except on the most superficial level. Sometimes the only escape from the image imposed on us – by the world, by ourselves finally – appears to be death.

So, then, what is that image? Twins as Freak Show in essence, I'm afraid – no more, no less. It's as Freak Show we make the eyes of the world light up; make the eyes of doctors (Mengele, for instance), of psychologists, mythologists, light up. Arguments about nature/nurture? The transmission of genetic diseases? Myths of dichotomy? Twins are the perfect research material. Of *course*. Naturally – and all unwittingly, as children – you play up to, go along with it. Others have to fight to get such attention. Twins, like royalty, don't have to fight – far from it. And just like royalty, discover the drawbacks, as against the unobtainable delights of anonymity, early on. Sure, everyone looks out for you. Sure, the headmistress of the school gets up and warns your fellows of your imminent arrival, and how you are to be treated like anyone else, and oh, please, addressed by your individual names, and not just called Twin. But of course at that point you don't mind being called 'Twin', that's what you're famous for; without reflection you accept the asking price, go on living up to images put forward, to the human need expressed in such images, which is why they are put forward in the first place. But God help you if you cling too long to the image forced on you. What is charming in the very young is freakish, to be abhorred, mocked at, in their elders. Once, in our local supermarket, I saw two elderly sisters, each with the same lank dark hair, streaked with grey, each wearing a dirty white raincoat, flat shoes, each with a headscarf in her left hand, and in her right a basket containing a bottle of Tizer and a packet of Cheddar cheese. After a certain age, in other words, no matter what you feel like, better to proclaim some kind of outward difference or risk remaining an object of the wrong sort of fascination. (Just

like Joan Collins, I can't help feeling; better for most of us
not to stay irrevocably twinned to our organs of generation,
either.)

Judging by the way twins remain such constant currency,
fascination – concerning twinship – is not too strong a
word. In the space of two weeks recently, television sched-
ules came up with *Dead Ringers* – psychic Siamese twins, in
the form of twin gynaecologists played by Jeremy Irons;
actual Siamese twins, heroes of an animated film; a programme about the twin survivors of Mengele's experiments
at Auschwitz; and – most bizarrely, because most unexpected – in an item about a protest march for pensioners
defrauded by Maxwell, a pair of identical elderly sisters, in
matching hairstyles and matching necktied bows, both of
whom happened to be Maxwell pensioners. Finally, for
good measure, there surfaced in London ten days later a
French opera – *Jumelles* – based on the story of June and
Jennifer, black twin arsonists, currently confined in
Broadmoor.

The piece about the Auschwitz twins impressed itself on
me most of all, as it was bound to. Only this morning, I
woke from a dream about twins, the nature of which I had
already forgotten. What I could not – cannot – forget,
though, was the cry I seemed to wake to: the cry from the
ramp at Auschwitz after a transport came in, and the
selections were being made, the cry by which Dr Mengele
gathered his research material: '*Zwillingen 'raus!*' 'Twins *out!*'

But then that's it; it's always a matter, in some sense, of
'*Zwillingen 'raus*'. Horrible as was the fate of many of the
Auschwitz twins, those who survived did so by virtue of
their twinship, the pure physical chance of having shared a
womb with someone else. Just because they were special –
in Mengele's eyes here – just because they were called
out, more of them survived, proportionately, than other

children sent to the camps. This particular curse – blessing – of specialness is something the survivors have had to spend the rest of their lives coming to terms with. They, even more than most of us, cannot escape their twinness. But none of us can really; all of us, in a sense, survive by virtue of what, often, we long to discard: the world's fascination with our duality.

An image, almost as telling, almost as painful as that evoked by '*Zwillingen 'raus*', came in the animated film about Siamese twins. They were a circus act, dancing as one, three legs between two, two arms between two, indissolubly united; in their dreams only were the pair divided. One saw himself as champion footballer; the other dreamed of pop stardom. In the end, grinning the desperate grin of the stage act, they are again performing – the audience is shown applauding, the performers applaud them, clapping the right – the only hand of one – on the left – the only hand of the other. What *fun*; couples in the audience, one by one, begin to link their redundant arms and use the left hand of the one, the right hand of the other, to applaud likewise; grinning away pleasure. For them it is a game, which, by performing as they are expected to perform – they are twins, aren't they? – the twins – who themselves, contrariwise, long to be separate – connive at. As all twins do in a way, as indissolubly linked psychically as Siamese twins are physically; even though this ideal, mimicked union is false at the heart; even though, as with those twins, our dreams, our hopes, are often different, and we find ourselves struggling, desperately, to tear ourselves apart.

In the case of the gynaecologists in the film *Dead Ringers*, the point was made precisely; at the climax one 'separated' himself physically by killing the other, using weird obstetric instruments designed for mutant physiology to make the analogy with birth quite clear. In my case, rebirth, separation, came rooted in a story which obsessed me as I emerged from the initial grief and shock of my twin's death: the story of the juniper tree, in which a tree grows, a bird sings on the tree, above the grave of a brother, as if the flesh and blood and bone fertilized the rebirth, the re-forming of identity. The image is terrible, yet exhilarating at one and the same time, just because it is so vividly cannibalistic; the very same image, the same power, is invoked, of course, in the Christian Eucharist. It's an image shocking, I've noticed, to non-Christians, who have not been brought up to take the intonings of 'with my body', 'with my blood' for granted, thereby forgetting – how could decorous Anglicans not forget? – the actuality of the rituals so invoked, the life-giving power of another human body ingested literally or symbolically to bring about spiritual or even physical regeneration. But I could not forget it, not through the terrifying, painful, yet lively months in which I felt myself in some way to be ingesting, taking life from, the decaying body of my sister, my womb-fellow. This is the only difference, I think, in the end, once the sense of loss is stripped down to its roots, between the grief of sibling for sibling and twin for twin: a sense of physical connection so strong that when one body dies you have either to rot with it or, in some psychic respect, to eat it.

(But then that's pretty much what you must do at the menopause, come to that. Indeed, for me, I realize, the one metamorphosis has transformed itself into an image – the image – of both. Coming to terms with the physical change, the menopause, means coming to terms with the psychic change: the loss of my sister; of my twoness. Each process as physical, as bloody as its twin.)

As I have said, my sister and I were not strictly identical, albeit alike enough to play the confusion game, at least as children. But as non-identical twins, we also lived out that other intrinsic image of twinness – opposites; the seduction of the dichotomy; left hand/right hand; dark/light; good/evil; rational/intuitive; arts/sciences; raw/cooked. And so on. People love dichotomies – it is significant, I daresay, that certain epileptic syndromes, certain psychoses, manifest themselves as obsession with them. And that, once again, trapped us. Some opposites we were, undeniably – she was right-handed, for instance, I left-handed; she an early sleeper and early waker; I in each case a late one (meaning that when, as children, we shared a bedroom, I was the one who read with a torch under the bedclothes at night, she the one who woke up and read early in the morning – something else we fought about constantly). Yet many of our differences were willed, chosen, rather than intrinsic, let alone natural. What's more, they were chosen very often, particularly in her case, in order to make a difference between us – not because we were actually different; any more than in our sameness we were actually the same. Even asserting our differences demonstrated, still, that each of us defined herself in relation to the other one, not to something intrinsic to our separate selves.

This is not to say we *weren't* different; from infancy, more or less, she trailed behind, picking up what I dropped; on which I capitalized, of course; never forced to find out whether I could be as good at picking up after her if it came to it. What it did come to was that I developed early a taste for being looked after, she for looking after people – something that stood her in poor stead in her final illness, when it would have done her no harm to look after herself rather better than she did. (That's something else that fills me with fury; I'm told it shouldn't, that she was what she was, I shouldn't expect her to have behaved as I might. But how can I not be angry with her for not behaving in a way that might have helped her live longer? – and me to feel less guilty about the fact she didn't, come to that.) As for me, it hardly turned me into the paragon wife and mother we were both reared to be. But that might have had some advantage in the way it also left me, who expects at heart still to be looked after, with the capacity to shrug off – quite ruthlessly sometimes – the demands of people who expect me to look after them. Such ruthlessness is essential for a writer, it helped me to be a writer; just as her tending helped to turn her into the genius she was at sorting out other people. Neither of us, we admitted at our best moments – sometimes – would have wanted the other's life; at the same time as each of us, in some respects, continued to judge our own against it.

I don't really know if my twin and I liked each other as children – it was not a question I think it would have occurred to either of us to ask. We certainly didn't always like each other as adults. But then liking never did have much to do with love; we loved each other about as much, often, as we appeared to hate each other. And though, as we grew older, even from seven or so, we adopted different friends, different activities – she was much the more gregarious of the two, I stayed by myself, reading – up till late adolescence we fought any more serious attempts to separate us. It was only at eighteen, finally, that we went our separate ways; she, as would prove to be usual, had much the worst of this development. I went to university, a move which took much of our parents' dwindling resources. She, no less intelligent, but having talents – scientific, rational – not catered for in our arts-orientated girls' school, was sent to secretarial college in the next town, rather than to London, as our parents had intended before my university fees ate up their spare funds. The guilt this engendered on the one side, the resentment on the other, festered through the rest of our lives; twins cannot help comparing not only themselves but the justice meted out to them, no matter what. My sister went to university later, as a mature student; but she did it, as she did most things, relative to me, the hard way. I was always the one who fell on her feet; my survival as against her death merely confirmed the pattern. As for my sister, not only did she not fall on her feet – at times, it seemed to me, she went out of her way to shoot herself in them. Often it came to seem almost a perverse opposition, yet another way of being different from me at all costs; fatally in the end, if you think of it like that, which I cannot always help doing.

A few weeks before she died – she was expected to last quite a bit longer than she did – she and her husband decided a charming kitten or two would comfort and enliven her sickbed. So off they went to Animal Rescue, and returned not with two friendly infant creatures, but with a pair of semi-feral, adolescent females, five months old at least. Both disappeared instantly under her bed, hissing, spitting and clawing at anyone who tried to make them come out. Only when she left the room did they emerge, to piss – and worse – all over the carpet. One of them ventured further, after she died. It escaped the house, a car hit it; I found its corpse in the ditch outside her gate. The pain at the loss of bleeding, the regret for the fate of my hormones, is nothing compared to the pain, the regret, I feel even now remembering that wretched little body – it was the black one, God knows what happened to its spotted twin – let alone the pain, the regret, I felt on seeing it in the ruthless brightness of that April morning. My sister, I thought, starting with me, going on with her men friends mostly, not least her two husbands – but that's another story – continuing with her probationers, her drug addicts, her alcoholics, ending up with her own menopausal, tumour-ridden body, always had set herself to succour hopeless cases.

John Timbers

COMING TO TERMS
Eva Figes

Being initiated into the mysteries of womanhood is associated in my mind with passing my Eleven Plus. What should have been a joyous, liberating moment was turned into something rather more solemn when my mother sat me down, after carefully shutting the door to ensure privacy, and told me about monthly periods. I was, she said, about to associate with older girls, and she did not want me to get things wrong.

I remember this little pep talk because it was somehow symbolic of the way growing up into a woman was presented to me, of dark and awful mysteries which lay ahead. My mother's earnestness when talking of menstrual blood and my reproductive function was in sharp contrast to her attitude to my academic achievements, which were regarded with faint disapproval, as a freakish aberration likely to interfere with my development into normal womanhood. My prime destiny was to look after a husband and children, and knowing how to cook and wash up was far more important than anything I might learn at school.

Well, the bleeding started, and was a constant source of shame and embarrassment. But this, I was starting to learn as part of my secondary education, was only the beginning. Worse – much worse – lay ahead. I might get pregnant before matrimony, in which case I would end up like Tess in *Tess of the D'Urbervilles*, a novel which scared the living daylights out of me.

My body was clearly a very dangerous instrument, a time bomb waiting to betray me, to judge from the literature I was devouring. This portrayal of budding femininity was reinforced by my mother, who treated my lower regions with a good deal more concern than she ever treated the rest of me. I remember being told off for rubbing myself with a towel, though all I was doing was trying to get dry. I was mystified by this prohibition. I knew better than to think I could get pregnant from a bath towel, but might it damage my reproductive functions, or what? No explanation was forthcoming. As far as I was concerned it was all very tiresome, and the only good thing to be said for the menarche was being able to get off hockey.

But by now I had read enough women's magazines to realize that my problems were only just beginning. If I managed to stay out of trouble long enough to go to university and take a degree – which meant technical virginity, since birth control was veiled in secrecy and was not part of either school or home education (in fact I came to the conclusion that my mother scarcely knew a thing about it herself, other than that it did not work); if I negotiated marriage and childbirth successfully and in the right order, a dreadful fate still awaited me, lay in store for all women: THE MENOPAUSE. An end to the painful, smelly business should be a reward for good behaviour, but apparently it was not. The Almighty really had it in for the daughters of Eve.

But it was not in my nature to be either fearful or docile – not at eighteen or thereabouts. It became clear to me that I was a new sort of woman, quite unlike my mother's generation. I had intellect, I had ambition, and I had no intention of turning into a domestic drudge. I also thought – and there were always those in the media who encouraged one to think – that the physical terrors which were woman's gynaecological lot were largely in the mind, and could be conquered. This, I think, was part of the ethos of the 1950s, when psychoanalysis was fashionable and doctors thought themselves invincible, so that any symptoms they could not alleviate tended to be diagnosed as psychosomatic.

For example, a fad called 'Natural Childbirth' was going the rounds about the time I gave birth to my first child. I remember seeing a short film in the cinema about a woman giving birth with this ecstatic look on her face: not a cry, not a whimper, passed her lips. I bought this hook, line, and sinker, and went into the labour room confident and smiling. The smile was soon wiped off my face as I went through the worst twenty-four hours of my life, during which I realized that childbirth was natural all right, but it was red in tooth and claw, and had absolutely no respect for my person. My vision of life changed utterly in those hours, and I knew now that whatever I might be as a person, as a woman I had simply become a vehicle, a pod, to be used and perhaps discarded after the event.

So now I knew about childbirth: the end result might be worthwhile, but the process was cruel. I also came to realize that, far from trumpeting their woes in a hysterical female fashion, there was really what almost amounted to a conspiracy of silence among women on the agonies of the labour room. My mother-in-law, mother of five, had said vaguely, during my first pregnancy, 'It's not as bad as they say', but in fact nobody had said anything much, except the American gentleman who invented Natural Childbirth and, like a fool, it was him I listened to. My own mother kept mum, except to say, when she came to see me in the hospital after the birth of my second child: 'The pains are worse the second time, aren't they?' Yes, they had been.

As a would-be writer, I now had something to write about. In the intervals between contractions when my first child was born I suddenly understood that the conspiracy of silence extended to the world's literature. This earth-shattering function, which made sexual love seem merely an *hors d'œuvre* for the meal itself, a bland prelude to the real business of living, had not even been touched upon in imaginative literature, let alone explored. What had induced women writers to keep silent for so long? I had the answers, and knew the time had come to speak out.

So now I knew all about menstruation and childbirth. This left one last hurdle in the dreadful gynaecological trilogy which makes up the life cycle of the human female: the menopause. But about this I was much more confident. Oh yes. As a divorced career woman, I felt myself well equipped to cope.

Well, obviously women had to accept the loss of their looks, which might be difficult. But if women experienced serious problems during the change, it was because they had stupidly opted for domesticity instead of a fulfilling career. Their children had left home, leaving them without a meaningful function, and their husbands no longer desired them, had perhaps turned to younger women. It sounds logical, and sometimes the logic undoubtedly fits.

But I suspect that feminists, particularly when they are young, and inexperienced, and full of optimism, have a deep inner need to deny that biology is destiny – partly because a woman's body is such a bind, and partly because men have always kept women suppressed, using biology as an excuse. Most of us know that the menstrual cycle affects our moods. When, in court, it is used as a mitigating circumstance to explain violent behaviour, we sympathize. Getting a murder charge reduced is one thing, getting paid less is quite another, so we tend to be ambivalent about the extent to which our hormones affect our ability to function.

As long as men hold the central positions of power, and go on providing the psychological 'norm' of what a working life is and should be, women's hormones are liable to go on being something of an embarrassment. This, of course, is ludicrous. For every woman who loses her temper as a result of PMT, there are dozens of men lashing out and causing grievous bodily harm as a result of their much-vaunted testosterone-based aggression. Our prisons are full of them; their macho hormones cost the taxpayer billions. Our social values are so man-orientated that we forget this. What we remember is a two-thousand-year-old philosophy, stretching back to Aristotle, which tells us that the soul of man resides in his logical brain, whilst that of woman is located in the womb, the source of hysteria.

I do not think biology is destiny, but I do think it has to be taken into account. The body is often a nuisance; it has its own agenda, which is not necessarily ours. We all learn this as we get older. One way or another we have to compromise, accommodate our wishes and desires to a stern and often unpredictable host. It is right to begin life full of optimism, to think positively, but it is downright silly to think that we were created by a Being who is egalitarian, non-sexist, and would – given a chance – vote Labour.

Still, feminism – unlike other political ideologies – has made genuine progress. Our gynaecological bits will always be a nuisance at times, but at least we now have some control over them. The menopause *does*, for many women – including yours truly – interfere with the body's thermostat, cause palpitations and insomnia, but a woman can now choose, within certain parameters of risk, to alleviate the symptoms by taking HRT. Nobody is forcing her to take anything, but she is permitted to make an informed choice.

I think we have come a long way. It is only a hundred years, after all, since doctors were adamantly opposed to birth control – not because of any genuine risks (at a time when thousands of women were dying in childbirth) but because constant childbearing was good business for the medical profession. There are still many problems to be overcome in the field of obstetrics and gynaecology, still so dominated by men, but I do not think HRT is an area of particular concern. There may be undiscovered risks, but this applies to every area of medicine and every pharmaceutical product. Life is a chancy business, and we do the best we can.

There is a tendency to regard the menopause as a phase which will pass, and pass more quickly if we do not interfere with nature. But it is no such thing: it is part of the ageing process, and goes on relentlessly. Women who had hot flushes at fifty will still be getting them at sixty, the bones that began thinning then will go on getting thinner, until the inevitable fractures start. The sleep of youth will not return. Far from being a problem for the bored housewife, as I once imagined, it now seems to me much more of a problem for the busy professional woman who wants to get on with her life, only to find her body playing stupid tricks on her. And women who are fortunate enough to suffer no symptoms should not presume to preach to the many who do. Experience in childbirth also varies widely, but nobody regards an easy, uncomplicated delivery as the norm.

Quite apart from the fact that HRT is now thought to reduce the danger of strokes by 50 per cent, and that one woman in four will develop osteoporosis after the menopause, it makes sense to go for the quality of life at this stage. It also makes sense to choose hormones rather than resort to sleeping pills or tranquillizers, and it certainly seems safer and more judicious to take hormone pills in the last two decades of your life span, when you are anyhow liable to all the ills that woman is heir to, than to start swallowing contraceptive pills shortly after puberty, with the whole of your life still ahead. At fifty you know yourself to be mortal, you have already seen many of your friends die, and you know that the risks of contracting a terminal disease increase with each passing year. If you are lucky enough to go on, you want to get the best out of every moment. Few people choose not to fly because of the risk involved, or suffer a headache if painkillers can get rid of it. The quality of life is what counts, and it counts even more when old age and death stare us in the face.

The quality of life. Suddenly, at fifty, I found myself enjoying a great sense of freedom, of serenity. It was the exact opposite of the panic and neurosis usually associated with the menopause. The change in me was so striking and consistent that I found myself saying: So *this* is women's liberation. And I knew my independence as a younger woman had been a charade – or rather, it was an independence of responsibility: for my children, my finances, my career. Perhaps, too, I could claim to have stood on my own feet intellectually, to have had the courage of my own convictions, regardless of profit or fashion. Beyond that, however, I had not been truly free, but a victim of my own emotions.

All my life, ever since puberty struck and I found myself spellbound by the handsome eyes of the English master, I had been falling in and out of love as predictably as the changing seasons: dewy-eyed with the first apple blossom, counting my losses, as likely as not, as trees shed their fading leaves. Well, not every year, of course, but when you do a fast rewind of your life, it seems very like it. Often I was in love with the idea of love rather than the person, since a life devoid of romance is like food without seasoning. Or it could be a fantasy, a possibility at the back of my head.

Either of these would be relatively harmless; chaos really set in when an actual involvement occurred. Suddenly I was no longer a free agent. We all know the sort of thing. Being rung up at the wrong time, or not at all. Putting holiday arrangements on hold, for too long. Putting friends on hold with insincere excuses. Letting career opportunities go, or not enjoying them. Generally being a puppet on invisible strings. It may be worth it, or pure hell. Often it is both. But whatever the profit and loss account shows, freedom it is not.

I think one can still fall in love after the menopause, but it will be different in quality: more of a gentle glow than a fiery furnace. The dying embers can be fanned in the right circumstances, but are unlikely to consume. But in general, we are no longer driven by our hormones and I, for one, find this an immense relief. We like to make a division between mind and body, spiritual and physical hunger, but we are really fooling ourselves if we think sex is not the driving force which impels us into the arms of another. It can bring joy, but is often irrational and destructive.

With this release from hormonal compulsion comes another, perhaps greater, release: we can stop worrying about the way we look. Gone is the struggle to attract with ever-decreasing physical assets, the possibility of humiliation. Gone, too, are the days of fending off unwelcome attentions from strangers, shrugging off clumsy approaches, pretending not to notice all those staring eyes. To become suddenly invisible may be disturbing at the age of forty, but now it strikes me as a blessing.

It is only women who have made a career of trading on their sex appeal who face a problem, and their efforts are often pathetic. They present a travesty of their former self to the world, invite ridicule, and fight an exhausting war they must ultimately lose. Because serenity, if it comes with the change, is not simply a release from sexual appetite. It has to do with accepting our own mortality, coming to terms with ageing and death. If we cannot do the latter, we are likely to go into a false frenzy with regard to the former – clutch at a toy boy, wear clothes too young for us, or agonize over the loss of a lover or husband without stopping to assess just what we are losing. Men of a certain age are physically attracted to younger women, and can be callous about leaving an older partner. But often that woman lost physical interest in him long ago, has been pleading the proverbial headache for years. Many wives have turned a blind eye to their husbands' infidelities, have even felt themselves relieved from an onerous connubial duty, just as long as they could keep the social and economic status which went with the marriage.

I am not minimizing the distress suffered by an ageing wife discarded for a younger model, simply trying to analyse the reasons for it a little more closely. Is she afraid of losing a lifelong companion, or the partner who makes it safe for her to negotiate the outside world? She has never entered a room, sat down at a formal dinner table, or gone to a reception except as her husband's wife. Travelling for pleasure without him seems an impossibility, even if their holidays were regularly marred by bickering or long silences. As for the physical side, it is bound to get a bit tiresome after twenty or thirty years. She would as soon get a good night's sleep.

And then there is the question of the meal ticket, more important than anything else when the chips are down. Fat, ugly men with bald heads and paunches, old as Methuselah, are able to attract females young enough to be their daughters if they are sufficiently famous, or have money, power, influence or talent. These attributes are, however, essential, since unemployed bricklayers of a certain age are not noted for pulling younger birds and, if their marriages end, it is usually because the wife throws them out. This raises the interesting question as to whether, once it is normal for a woman to be a high achiever, she too will find bliss in the arms of a younger man.

At present social attitudes militate against this. Men like to be in control, and they feel awkward with powerful and intelligent women who do not defer to them. 'Toy boy' is the jokey expression. The stereotypes may pass away, but is there a deeper reality which will prevail, and determine sexual relationships? A woman's sexual desire can be faked; she can fool her partner and even herself. But a man cannot pretend arousal; his instrument will let him down. At the level of selfish gene theory, a man can beget children by a younger woman, but a woman past the menopause will never conceive, so nature has decreed that useless effort is avoided. It is not that an older man desires to father ever more children – many men in second marriages find their young wives' desire for children a distinct handicap at an age when they would rather doze in front of the television set. But his body automatically responds to young and fertile flesh, and intellect hardly comes into it.

This is unfair, but does it really matter if a woman is self-reliant and successful? Most women know that they cannot 'have it all' in this world: that fulfilling career ambitions always seems to demand sacrifices of a kind which men in similar situations are not required to make. They spend the best years of their lives juggling the demands of home and career, and something usually gets lost on the way. The chance of a lifetime, the love of a lifetime, or just that indefinable something called contentment.

And then, one day, contentment comes. It comes in the shape of the menopause. She is fifty, her children have left home and given her a breathing space. Her career, such as it is, has reached its plateau, so she can stop striving – if it is not quite what she had dreamed of, it is too late to kick against the pricks now. Is there a man in her life and, if not, does it matter? She may be alone, but she is no longer lonely, since her body no longer craves what she cannot have. She may have the companionship of a long-standing partner, or, like many women at this stage of their lives, suddenly realize that this partnership has become a hollow sham, and end it. She may even find herself a new partner, offering true companionship for her remaining years. And she can, either way, stop the exhausting struggle of keeping up appearances, now that it no longer matters, and she no longer cares. Oh, the joy of invisibility, of grey hair and wrinkles, spectacles and comfortable shoes! Of seeing, rather than being seen!

This is a time when a woman, with luck and good sense on her side, comes into her own. This is the time, if she has come to terms with her own mortality, when she can really savour the moment, the passing day, the gift of every hour. She knows that time is not limitless, and this makes it precious. Everything she has is now, and she must make the most of it. Her body has been liberated from foolish longings, and perhaps she should find it in her heart to pity the men of her generation who are led by their penises into all kinds of foolishness, sordid hanky-panky which exposes them to ridicule, or demanding second marriages which exhaust them both physically and financially.

And then the menopause is a kind of autumnal gift. Until this century so many women died as a result of childbearing that very few of them ever reached it – to previous generations it must have seemed almost like getting to heaven, or at least a safe haven. Medically, it is a modern problem, and modern medicine is now helping us to deal with it positively rather than negatively, so that we can make the most of our autumnal years.

The sense of coming to terms with death which coincides with the menopause is the real breakthrough, enabling us to achieve contentment and serenity. Our children do not so much bury us as push us aside, out of the limelight. Suddenly the world is a foreign country, full of young people with odd hairstyles, speaking a language we scarcely comprehend. It makes it easier to go, and from the age of fifty one sees the world with valedictory eyes. There is nothing morbid about this, it is just the way it is. Many of our friends have already left, and it may be our turn soon.

Not since early childhood have I lived so fully in the moment, savouring small things. I am not under pressure, and the changing sky beyond my study window, or the trees beneath, have my full attention. I fiddle with a pot plant which has just burst into bloom, or try out the piano, newly tuned. I have a little grandchild who gives me enormous joy but, thankfully, she is somebody else's responsibility. And my writing has also changed, though until I found myself writing this I had not made a connection, and there may not be any. I only know I worry less, trust my skill and intuition more: knowing I can swim, I plunge fearlessly into deep water.

I know I must soon face deep water of another kind and hope, as we all do, that the tide, when it comes, will be reasonably gentle. Meanwhile I sit on the beach, letting sand sift through my fingers, watching the light change, the passing clouds. It is all so new for my granddaughter. I would like to gather seashells for her, put one to her ear, and watch the expression of wonder on her face.

Tara Heinemann

HOW WAS IT FOR YOU?
Margaret Forster

My mother never mentioned the word 'menopause' to me, but then she did not mention a great many other words: periods, menstruation, puberty, sex, womb . . . There was a whole hidden vocabulary learned later from friends and books. She used to send me, as a young child, to a shop nearby with a note which said: 'One packet of Dr White's, please'. I'd be given a plain brown paper package which I would trot home with, not having the least idea what was in it. I asked, of course, being an intensely curious child, and was told either 'Things' or 'You'll know in good time', both of which answers drove me mad.

When I was ten, and my mother was forty-six, the collecting of the mysterious packages stopped. My mother went into hospital for 'an operation', and when she came out she never needed me to go again. Naturally, I'd no idea what the operation was for. 'Something inside,' I was told.

The more I pressed to be told exactly what, the more distressed my mother became. So I stopped asking. I watched her with great anxiety instead. She put on weight rapidly, after always being slim, and her hair seemed to turn white in the space of a few months. She was depressed, even melancholic, but then she often had been. Whatever it was that had happened inside was obviously not good news.

Another word was added to those not used: 'hysterectomy'. I heard a neighbour say, 'Well, you were at the change anyway, so what's the odds?' It sounded such an unemotive word that I risked asking, 'What's the change?' 'Nothing,' I was told.

But do not deduce from this that my mother was a silly or ignorant woman. On the contrary, she was highly intelligent, one of that generation of working-class women who were cheated of the higher education they should have had (and which we, their daughters, then received). So the explanation for why she kept everything to do with menstruation virtually secret had more to do with psychological reasons than anything else. She believed, I think (because it was never discussed), that talking about 'intimate problems' was somehow indelicate. It upset her without her being able to say why. There was embarrassment and even misplaced pride mixed up in her furtive attitudes – she wanted this side of her life ignored, to pretend it did not exist.

Now this had a good as well as a bad effect on me. The bad effect is all too obvious and hardly needs to be stated, but the good effect was more subtle. Because my mother believed in concealing everything to do with menstruation, including its ending, the menopause, it never loomed large in my thoughts. My mother did not moan and groan every month or fill me full of dire warnings about pains and aches and floodings and all the other things many of my friends' mothers frightened them with. I grew up believing this 'something' that happened to women could be risen above and need not feature too much in their lives. I had no fear of the menopause because I did not associate it with my mother after her operation. This operation was one thing; the aftermath, during which she visibly aged, another. I made no connection.

This attitude to the menopause continued after I left home and right up to my own menopause. I never had the slightest fear of it; it didn't loom over me or cause me any apprehension. But I was aware, all the same, that I was ridiculously ill-informed: I really hadn't the faintest idea what happened beyond periods stopping. I'd slide my eyes occasionally over articles in newspapers and magazines to do with the menopause, but never had the interest I had in similar features about, say, pregnancy. As far as I was concerned, it was just something that happened naturally and I couldn't see any reason to worry about it until it happened, and preferably not even then.

So I went into my own menopause quite blithely. I first thought it might be starting when, over a year, my periods were not only lighter and shorter but had longer gaps between them. Well, thought I, if this is the jolly old menopause then hurrah. I was forty-six at the time, the same age my mother had her strange operation, and I found myself wondering why she had had what I by then knew was a hysterectomy. (She was dead, so I couldn't ask.)

The next thing that signalled a menopause in progress was faint – *very* faint – feelings of heat in the face and neck. It took me quite a while to realize these were the famous hot flushes of all the jokes, and once more I was amazed at how harmless they were. And so I found myself wondering, at the age of forty-seven, when menstruation had ceased, in the immortal words of Bob Geldof, 'Is that it, then?'

For me it was, but I don't make the mistake of deducing

that the menopause is a doddle for everyone. Mine was, yours might be, but certainly others' won't be. Like childbirth, it's all a matter of luck, or a great deal of it. I have had three children and know very well how violently different the experience of giving birth can be, ranging from simple and ecstatic to absolute torture and horrible complications. The menopause, that other great female watershed, is the same: some, like me, sail through it, hardly aware it is happening; others have their lives wrecked. But so vociferous are those who back HRT that it is perhaps worth reminding women that they ought at least to wait and see before embarking on it. Nature, sometimes, can manage perfectly well on its own.

Even easier to manage, for me, has been the transition to post-menopausal woman – but then, again, I would say that, wouldn't I? If I had had no children, and had wanted them, then the menopause would have been a time of wistfulness, and perhaps even real despair. Fine for me that my childbearing years are over – I was actually glad to see them go. It struck me as wonderfully neat that just as my children were all more or less off on their own I should suddenly be given all this extra energy to work harder and better than I had ever been able to. During my premenopausal years I was so often exhausted, whereas in my post-menopausal ones I am rested and fitter. I'm able to be so good to myself. A little tired? Fine, I put my feet up and read a novel in the middle of the day if I want to. I am another creature, and the physical benefits are enormous.

But of course, so far as looks go – ah, looks! – I am also another creature, and have to face up to it. Face is the word. I've never in my life worn make-up of any sort, so there is nothing to hide behind. The lines and wrinkles are there, and sometimes I do catch sight of myself and get a slight shock. Whether, after I've recovered, I mind or not is difficult to answer truthfully. On balance, I have to admit I *do* mind, and that I do regret the disappearance of a smooth skin and good complexion, but what I do *not* mind so much is what it signifies – I don't mind looking like what I am: a middle-aged woman. If, when young, I had been beautiful or glamorous, then I think I would have been depressed by the change in my facial appearance – hard, surely, to have had a lovely, glowing face and then have to adapt to wrinkled skin. Older faces can have a beauty of their own, and glow in a different way, but they are not attractive in the *same* way.

And this, of course, is what is regarded as the crux: attraction. Post-menopausal women are thought of as not sexually attractive, and that is what they are supposed to mind most of all. It is no good wheeling out Joan Collins or Jane Fonda or Cher because the whole point of women like that is that they attempt to defy the menopause and stay young-looking and therefore, allegedly, attractive. But women who do that are exactly those women whose whole life has been built on this physical attraction of theirs. Mine has not been. If I'm attractive to the one man who loves me, and whom I love, and am attracted by, then the rest of the world doesn't matter.

But there we go again – luck. If there was no one man with whom I was able to be so secure, then my whole perspective might change. I could not be so relaxed about the lines, the general ageing, if I had to go out into the world and hope to attract. And some women do have to, and want to, do that – post-menopausal or not. Sex can't simply be cut out of one's life because one is post-menopausal, even if it is true – which I think it is – that it occupies a different place.

This is certainly the aspect of the menopause talked about least – something not quite nice about thinking about sex and the menopause, it seems. Germaine Greer got it only half-right in *The Change*, and the half she got wrong was dangerous. It is not, as she suggested, that post-menopausal women should rejoice because sex means nothing to them any more, but that they should recognize it doesn't mean the same. Sex doesn't dominate life as it used to, nor is the need for it so intense, but it does not disappear, nor are its pleasures and joys gone for ever. I think there *is* some sadness in this, but it's tolerable just so long as paradise can be regained sometimes.

As in so many parts of ageing, nature tries to help by arranging for what would, at one stage of life, be far, far too little to be sufficient. It is not so much the waning of desire as the spacing of it. The bit Germaine Greer got right was how satisfactory it is not to be dictated to by hormones *all the time* so that nothing else mattered, for so many years, but sex.

Other things now matter just as much, and one of them is work. Throughout my adult life I've had to scheme and battle to find time and energy to work. I got married young, at twenty-two, and had children young: my first at twenty-five. My first novel was published weeks before my first child was born. For the next twenty years it was a case of the familiar juggling act: wife, mother and, trailing a poor third, writer. I chose this. I wanted this. I regretted none of it. I wouldn't have had it any other way. But the fact remains that, self-inflicted or not, the load was heavy, and carrying it was a strain.

In my own case I made it heavier than it might have been and the strain greater by doing everything myself without help – no cleaners, no nannies, no au pairs. But equally, the consequence of the load being lifted, because it was so heavy, was dramatic. I am thrilled with my post-menopause status so far as work goes. I find my output has doubled and I love saying 'yes' to things when always before I had to say 'no' because one more job and I'd have cracked. And because I am suddenly available I am more in demand:

certainly I can whip in today and do a review for 'Kaleidoscope'; a pleasure to take part in a 'Bookshelf' discussion; absolutely no problem about appearing in a book programme on some TV channel.

Naturally, when I get to these places, all the producers are younger. Much younger. Young enough to be my children exactly. This could make me feel an Old Bat. But it doesn't – or rather, it does, but I like it. These young things have enthusiasm and energy which, you would suppose, would be matched by my – perhaps – experience and gravitas – but not at all. Yes, I do have experience and a certain weight which comes from it, but I've never yet found any of them outstripped me for enthusiasm or intellectual energy.

That, yet again – and I never forget it – is my luck: to have work which takes virtually no regard of age. A literary critic is, if anything, of *more* value older rather than younger. The younger critic, inevitably, has a mark to make, and wants to make it; the older critic doesn't have to worry, and can enjoy herself more. And I cannot deny that I like being thought of as dependable, as professional, because I've been tried and tested. They know what I can do, and this leads to a lovely welcome.

When I was young and a slashing attacker, at times the tension could be acute on both sides. I'd be worked up because I wanted to blast something, and the producer would be anxious I'd overdo it. All that has gone from this fringe work of mine. It is a pure pleasure, and has become that only with age.

One thing that has not yet come with age – and it is something heavily associated with menopausal women – is the change of status from mother to grandmother. I am not, thank heaven, a grandmother, though most of my contemporaries are. I don't say 'thank heaven' because the thought of being a grandmother depresses me – on the contrary, I'm sure I'd love it – but because none of my children seems to me anything like ready to have children.

But I don't find, as people seem to expect me to, that I yearn for grandchildren. I don't think this is an automatic part of being post-menopausal – unable to breed myself, but wanting my children to do it for me. I haven't become in the least haunted by visions of myself holding a beloved grandchild. In a way I feel I want the gap: motherhood is only just over, in the practical if not emotional sense, and I'm in no hurry to start grandmotherhood even if it is – or so I'm told – not so arduous and all-consuming a calling.

It may also be because I relish what I am at the moment, more my own person than I have ever been. 'Fifty is the heyday of a woman's life,' said Elizabeth Cady Stanton, one of the early-nineteenth-century feminists. It feels my heyday. What surprises me is the increase of my sense of ambition: I thought it would desert me, but it hasn't. I've always been ambitious, but during my childbearing years I could feel this desire to write a great book fading away, becoming unimportant beside the bearing and rearing of children. There was some definite loss of motivation. What was a book, after all, compared to a child? How could I want to be a good writer when it was so much more absorbing and gratifying trying to be a good mother?

But the ambition came back as my youngest child reached around thirteen, and now it is fierce again. Curiously, it doesn't yet seem to dismay me that I haven't fulfilled this ambition – I simply like having it. I don't, as a writer, have to look at myself only halfway up a ladder, as I would have to if I were in another profession, and see that at my age I'll now never reach the top. That probably would depress me, and I'd see the menopause as an awful tolling of a bell telling me I was doomed never to reach my potential. But no bells toll for writers, not until the final hour of their lives.

Nor does that final hour, or its approach, cause me much

concern. When I was young, I thought about death a great deal. Now, when it is bound to be so much nearer, I rarely think of it, and when I do it is without fear. For the post-menopausal woman, with this 'dying' of one part of herself, this running down of a system which has operated for some forty years, there should be an inescapable sense of being reminded that death is coming. But I don't feel it. I don't believe I am blocking out or suppressing fears of death so much as appreciating and revelling in all that feels vigorously alive in myself.

The menopause has brought with it a better adjustment to myself, and I'm grateful for it. I haven't found myself an easy person to live with, ever – too irritable, too demanding, too impatient, too critical, too moody; the list is endless. I've spent far too many years wishing I was different, and some few trying to make myself so, all to no avail. Now, I've accepted myself and I get on with myself better. This may very well be due to hormonal changes; if so they happened naturally, and I'm charmed by them. If they do exist, these changes, and had not happened for me, and if as a result I'd been even more irritable, and so on, then maybe I would have tried HRT.

I am not entirely anti-HRT, but I am very wary of how it is used – of the propaganda, if you like. If a woman has appalling menopausal symptoms, then fine, try it, but what I cannot go along with is its use *before* any symptoms have appeared in order to 'stay young'. The idea is that 'We all want to stay young and sexy if we can,' said Teresa Gorman (to me, during a television discussion). But no, I don't think that we all either do or should.

What we *do* all want to do is not suffer terrible hot flushes, sweats and all the other things I never had, but neither do we (or some of us) want to use drugs, for ever, to evade the appearance of growing old. That is to falsify ourselves in the worst possible way, to place an even greater emphasis on looks than there already is. The menopause would then become a time when the great pretence would have to begin and be maintained until death – and death not even HRT could halt.

It would also rob me, at least, of the benefit of looking an older woman. I love the fact that my obvious age makes me reassuring and trusted. I have clearly 'seen life', and this draws forth all kinds of confidences and requests for advice. I love it. I've always liked listening to anyone's problems, but never have I had to listen so hard as during the last few years when suddenly I am meant to be wise, as befits my age. I have run the whole female race from start to finish, and this makes me useful to younger women. Howling babies? Troublesome teenagers? My dear, I've seen and dealt with the lot – just try me. On love affairs I am not so hot, only ever having had one, but even then I am a safe person to confide in, and ever ready to listen and come up with what I think is considered judgement.

And I love the young women who sometimes confide in me. I cannot imagine where this legendary competitiveness between younger and older women comes from, this jealousy there is supposed to be. 'You look beautiful,' I tell them, and, 'You're so talented,' I remind them, and, 'Go for it,' I urge. The young, instead of appalling me, or making me envious, fascinate me.

Sometimes, one of them will groan, 'I'll be thirty next year, oh *God*, thirty!' and I am reminded of the panic of youth. To be thirty and not to have achieved what one wanted – not, perhaps, to have got anywhere near it – is enough to make the blood run cold. At thirty, there is no way of knowing if whatever one wants ever will be gained, especially if it is to do with lovers and children. So I do not fool myself: I am relaxed, as a post-menopausal woman, because I am, on the whole, happy with how my life has turned out.

I remember, with pain, the unhappiness of women who, at the menopause, had to face the fact that life had *not* given them what they wanted. In those days, a mere forty years ago, there were so many more of them. Life was motherhood, put plainly. When the children left home, and especially if they moved away, all meaning in one's days was virtually over. My mother had no career: we were her career. When we left she felt useless. She joined various church clubs and tried to fulfil herself in other ways, but she did not succeed. The menopause to her meant the end of everything she cared about.

But my generation has been more fortunate. Most of us have careers of one sort or another, most of us have not been complete slaves to our children, most of us have worn better because our lives have been physically easier: we haven't scrubbed stone floors, stood over sinks washing clothes by hand, raked out fires, toiled home with heavy bags of shopping, or any of those other household tasks which aged women so. We have had infinitely better pregnancies and childbirths, and we have approached the menopause physically in far better shape.

All this should be something to rejoice over; it should remove the stigma of the dreaded menopause to know the better condition we are all in. But it has not done so – not yet. It amuses me, when I ask a contemporary, 'Are you through the menopause yet?', to be met quite often with the indignant reply, 'Certainly not!', as though I'd insulted her. No other inquiry of a middle-aged woman is so resented.

Nor does any, except the rare woman, ever advertise the fact that she *is* post-menopausal. Women will rush to tell you they are pregnant, or even to discuss miscarriages and abortions, but they seek to hide their menopauses. No one ever says, 'Isn't it great – I'm post-menopausal and I feel terrific.' If the menopause is talked about at all, it is in whispers, and always to complain.

Only the attitudes of women themselves can change this. The more women make it known that the process itself *can* be perfectly easy, and the change which takes place hugely beneficial, as well as nothing to fear, the more the menopause will cease to be a thing of dread.

The Desire to Create
Virginia Browne

'Did it bother you much?' my friend asked cosily. We were catching up on news after nine or ten years of being out of touch.

'The menopause?' I said, at the top of my voice. It tends to get away from me in unexpected crescendos when I get interested. 'Heavens no! I didn't notice it.'

'That's good news,' said her husband, walking in through the open door. 'I love coming home to items of news like that.'

Good news, but could it possibly be true news? I thought it was at the time of speaking, or yelling, but later I realized it couldn't have been; in fact I remembered noticing that I missed a month now and then and with increasing frequency, that the inconvenient, messy stream was growing mercifully thinner and briefer; and that all this had been happening for some months by the time it pushed its way into my consciousness. And when it did, did it really mean nothing to me? Of course not. When I looked for the memory it came back easily and clearly: the thought 'So the chance is over'.

Not a great sorrow, because the chance of having a child had always daunted rather than beckoned me. Until well after the great change I had found life very difficult, myself being one of its most difficult ingredients, and had known that I was too bad at handling it to make a good mother. Besides, I was sure to make an unhappy marriage, and that would make a child or children doubly difficult, a doubly fruitful source of guilt and disappointment. So, not a great sorrow; but a deprivation, a perceptible loss, bringing a sense of walls narrowing.

Too many easy generalizations are made about a woman's need to have a child. It's not a universal need, and among those who do share it the strength varies. I am one who shares or rather shared it, and one who has found the need tepid and fitful. Creating is certainly the most interesting thing in life to me, but creating of other kinds. As a child I played with dolls, but enjoyed reorganizing the dolls' house as a hospital more than the pram-pushing, the dressing and undressing and so on. Come to think of it, my pleasure in organizing must have amounted to a craving because I remember a pointless game I played alone for a whole week, distributing empty jars that had once contained malt and cod liver oil all over our large garden, putting rolled-up lumps of Plasticine into them in varying numbers, taking them from one assembly point to another, and yearning for the whole elaborate business to be *about* something. Three or four years later I went away to school, and was given more satisfying things to do and create. Carpentry became my passion. I was bad at it and knew it, but that didn't matter much. I saved up endlessly for a vice and a plane, and slept with Dryad's catalogue under my pillow.

Writing had begun early, as soon as I learnt to write and alas before I learnt to spell, which armed my family with a number of best-forgotten quotations. It too was a fitful need, and long before I got myself to work at it with any regularity I had had to choose some method of paying the rent. Like most teachers, including those of us who love teaching, I began by saying that I would do anything except teach. Schoolteaching would have come to an end within hours, when my pupils realized how raggable I was. University teaching is easier at any time, and in the late 1940s it was immeasurably easier. Most of the people reading for degrees in English Literature had fought in the war, and were old enough and battered enough to study seriously and have small interest in causing embarrassment. I was broken into teaching the kind way. What had begun as marking time while I waited for destiny held my attention for the best part of twelve years and then again, many years later, for another twenty, almost. It became clear after a while that teaching contained a creative element that made it more or less classifiable with carpentry and writing (and all too often almost identical with popping Plasticine pellets into empty cod liver oil jars). Something prevented it, unfortunately, from being embraced wholeheartedly: a suspicion, which quickly became a conviction, that literature should never be taught as exam fodder. It should be taught, of course, but no one should be in a position to know that if they remembered enough about certain books composed with the aim of entertaining and enlightening they would be able to get a job. To barter marks for observations on any work of art is a sort of blasphemy, besides inviting intellectual and emotional dishonesty.

It became necessary, therefore, to get out of a largely enjoyable racket, and I was able to become a teacher again only when the TEFL industry started up. Teaching English as a Foreign Language is more notoriously a racket than teaching Eng Lit, of course, or rather it is better known as a hotbed of rackety practices; there must be ten rip-off language schools for every one that does a thoroughly professional job. However, from the teacher's point of view – or from this teacher's point of view – the subject to be taught is wonderfully incorruptible, and stands up infinitely better to the wear and tear of repetitive lessons.

Between my Eng Lit and TEFL careers I did a number of other things, about 50 per cent of which were not in the least creative. Of those that were, producing radio programmes for the BBC was the most satisfying. It was creative in the way that teaching is: both producing and teaching, if done well, are in essence the art of enabling. There is a deep satisfaction in seeing learners become more interested, more aware, more confident, more capable of teaching themselves, less in need of a teacher. The teacher has to learn to do less and less of the talking, to guide only as much as is necessary, not to show off, not to interfere needlessly, not to deprive learners of making their own discoveries or correcting their own mistakes, not to pretend to know all the right answers. The teacher must try harder than most not to take a dislike to people, or to make cocksure interpretations of their behaviour. And the producer's job is much the same: to let people be themselves, discover ways of developing their self-confidence, avoid confirming their fears or making them feel they've trodden on a step that wasn't there. The producer must appear confident, so that the actors or speakers have the comfortable feeling that they're in safe hands, but mustn't be a know-all or a show-off, and above all must suppress any longing to be themselves the broadcaster, the highly original interviewer, the fascinating person who can show them all how it's done. The producer, like the teacher, must be curious to know what will emerge.

As a mother, presumably, is.

I ask myself if I stayed in teaching and then in radio production and once again in teaching for as long as I did because I couldn't commit myself to the more purely creative activities of motherhood or writing. The answer is yes, partly, but mostly because the first alternative would have involved too many unsatisfactory conditions and the second was no way to earn the rent. It must be admitted, though, that I undoubtedly let teaching and producing gobble up all my time and energy instead of leaving some for more purely creative activity. I wonder why.

Is any creative activity as purely creative as parenthood? Probably yes; probably nothing can properly be called purely creative, even parenthood. Becoming a carpenter, a writer, a teacher, a mother, is partly a matter of meeting social expectations. And how pure is the urge to create, in any of these ways? Is it not partly an urge to re-create yourself? Or to unburden yourself? Is there no wish to be heard and seen? No desire for success? Granted that all these play a part, what if none of them has been satisfied by the time the menopause tells you that the physical basis of your creativeness is no more? Do you then say: Oh well, the chance of those things, too, has gone? Or should you? I don't see why you should, and certainly you don't, most of the time.

As I write all this I'm continually amazed at myself for doing so, amazed that this book is being put together and published, will presumably be bought at bookstalls to be read on trains and planes. I should be used to this sort of thing by now, but I'm not. The people I grew up amongst had too strong a sense of privacy to talk about a subject of this kind. They had no objection to talking about death or religion, but I can't imagine any of the adults I knew before my mid-twenties (other than fellow students) talking about any aspect of sex. None of them would even have described someone as 'attractive'; my Victorian/Edwardian parents, aunts, uncles and similar described a personable young female as 'a jolly-looking gyal – such jolly looks', and a personable young male as . . . I forget, but certainly not 'attractive'. It was not merely that the word belonged to a vocabulary that they *considered* (but didn't *call*) common – or rather, 'vulgar'; it was simply not an aspect of people that they gave much thought to.

As to the powerful forces that give rise to attractiveness (or fail to), I don't think the adults of my childhood and youth were ignorant or afraid of them, but they didn't want to discuss them. It was not that they were repressed, or wanted to repress anyone else; I would say that their attitude to the assorted nature of human properties was simpler, more relaxed and more honest than that of people who want to 'take the lid off' this and that. To them, things had an inside and an outside; some human impulses and pre-occupations belonged in the public domain, others did not. Allowing what is considered private in most cultures to remain private was part of everyday good manners and, besides, it made occasional lid-lifting anything but banal.

In losing that attitude we have lost, I think, a great deal that is precious. There are many things I don't want to know about other people's lives, thoughts and habits, and would rather keep to myself about my own. When I'm watching or reading the story of two people's love, suspicion, competitiveness, understanding, misunderstanding, boredom, passion and affection, and suddenly find myself hauled into bed with them and obliged to stay there while they thrash about, I feel wild with irritation. Can't you keep *anything* to yourselves, you two? Is this carry-on anything *beyond* the lid-off bit? And if not, how much longer will it take to get the lid well and truly off this very widespread form of human behaviour? There is still, to me, a whole area surrounding it that should be entered from time to time, but always with care and respect. It still startles me to see words like *menstruation* and *menopause* on the printed page. And here I am causing them to be printed.

I felt this kind of shock, but stronger, when Mary, a friend and contemporary of my parents', said to me at fifty: 'I do think this business should have come to an end by now. It seems most unfair of God to let it go on when I've had six babies.' She was packing, and said this as she put a packet of sanitary towels into her suitcase, with me as a startled spectator. The first impact of her uncharacteristic lid-lifting soon faded, leaving me with something that was useful to me when I approached the same age. It was possible actually to *want* the menopause. An intelligent, achieving sort of woman could actually want to leave the childbearing years behind her and get into the next phase of her life. Remembering her, I thought: Well, so long as that hot flush business doesn't happen to me, I don't see why this should bother me.

The trouble is, people assume that it does bother you, that hot flushes and other less well-known symptoms are currently warping your temper and judgement and will continue to do so for some years. It's vexing to see, when you disagree with someone or criticize something, that people are thinking: Ah . . . she looks about . . . She must be going through a difficult time. There you are, quietly getting saner and saner, and they're discounting everything you say. When will people stop making allowances for you? The indefinite length of the treatment is one of its worst features.

But surely one *should* make allowances for someone who's going through the change of life? Yes. It's the same difficulty one has over someone who's disabled or married to an alcoholic or blighted by a horrible childhood or chronically unemployed: how to make fair-minded allowances without burying her under them.

To return to Mary, mother of six. In the fullness of time, God or Nature decided it was time to be fair and let her off the treadmill of preparing for a seventh. And how did she take it? With calm and interest. As far as I know she had no disturbing physical problems to deal with, and her change of outlook, though visible, appeared to result from a process of reassessment rather than renunciation. Her attitude towards her children and grandchildren became more detached, sometimes more detached than they liked. One of her sons was shaken when his request for advice on his new garden was not met as he expected. 'You're a great gardener, Mum. What are the key shrubs to plant, and where should they go?' – 'I don't know, darling. Do tell me what you decide.' While withdrawing much of her emotional investment from the stock of her middle years, she looked unhurriedly for alternatives. She began to paint for the first time in her life, learned German in preparation for her first visit to Germany, and made several new friends at an evening class. 'Of course I go to an evening class. It's always recommended. The menopause class.' Usually she called it 'the Phase One Elderberries', the Phase Two Elderberries being the Evergreen Club, which she joined twenty years later.

I shall soon be a Phase Two Elderberry myself. When I think about Mary, it seems to me that accepting membership should be like acceptance of that earlier and more concentrated change of life – a reassessment of what has so far been achieved and of what can still be done, a deliberate reshaping for anyone capable of it, and for no one a simple waiting to see what'll happen to you.

WALLS
Sara Banerji

To me the menopause is about walls.

I started my conscious life within a womb's walls, and my three daughters started theirs in mine. It is the physical and emotional realization that after the change of life these magical walls enclose rooms that are destined to be for ever empty that is supposed to make menopausal women sad. My womb, with its vital walls, protected me because as a woman I was spared certain dangers and burdens. Perhaps that is why, on the day when I walked into my own house for the first time, I patted the plaster with my hands and mumbled gleefully, if inanely, 'Mine, all mine'. I could do what I liked with these walls – even hammer nails into them if I wanted. That was forty years ago, and ever since my walls have been as studded with nails, nail holes, and plastered plugs as a punk's nostril. Until very recently I continued to view my blemished, used, hung-upon, pimpled walls with the tremendous satisfaction a victorious general must have when he contemplates enemy territory taken.

But walls imprison as well as protect. From my earliest years, the adult women of my life – nanny, mother, aunts, teachers – exhorted: 'Girls shouldn't carry heavy things.'

'Why?'

'It's bad for your womb.'

'What's a womb?'

'The container in which you will make babies when you are grown-up.' I understood then that it was for these future children's sake, not my own, that I must protect my body, and for several years I went around imagining an immature saucepan inside me waiting for the unexplained day when, like a simmered sauce or overcooked cabbage, a tender seasoned baby would emerge. My brother could take risks not open to me because I had to take care that my sensitive baby-maker did not get damaged.

No one explained what set the baby off in the first place, though I thought I knew. Nanny always counted how many damsons I ate, and made sure every stone came out again.

'What will happen if I swallow one?'

'It'll grow into a damson tree inside you.'

I supposed there must be some sort of similar pip which gave you a baby. The idea was not pleasant. Having my insides poked with damson twigs seemed only marginally more horrid than being piddled in by an unborn infant.

I was brought up by three sorts of women: mother, nanny, and nuns. To my mother, all women except herself had only a single function: to attract men and bear the children of one of them – 'men' because she was of the flapper generation, and admired women who were capable of multiple male conquests. I remember my mother asking my then teenage daughter, Sabita, why she was going out with only one young man.

'Because he's my boyfriend, Granny.'

'A granddaughter of mine should be capable of grabbing lots of young men, not just one. In my day I had dozens of boyfriends,' boasted Granny proudly.

'That's immoral, Granny,' gasped Sabita in horror.

I was a boarder at a series of convents in England, where the nuns were French; in Scotland, where they were English; and in Rhodesia, where they were German. The one thing they all had in common was their suspicion of human fertility and all that it entailed. We girls getting the curse was bad enough, and the nuns' fears were not unreasonable, for in my Rhodesian convent we had a glass window on the lavatory roof through which a girl changing her sanitary towel saw a man staring down on her. The episode resulted in some sort of sexual awakening for us. Our dormitory sister, a tiny nun in full Dominican habit, chased the man and grabbed him in a way that would have impressed my mother as he escaped over the convent wall. She managed to pull his shoe off, and from then on the reward for top behaviour was a glimpse of the 'sex maniac's' shoe.

Nanny had never managed to grab a man in any sense of the word, and was not religious either. For her, open bowels was the female objective.

During term I would be enthused with spirituality, vowing to give up the world and take the veil at the first opportunity, but during the holidays my ambitions would fluctuate between the bearing of children and the option offered by Nanny. My brother and I would discuss in fascinated whispers the various characteristics, colour, texture, of the products of diarrhoea and constipation, human by-products that seemed to us at the time no more disgusting – and rather more interesting – than babies.

Neither being a nun nor being a mother appealed to me, though in the end the latter began to seem the most realistic of my female options. Because of my mother's complaints

I was aware of children's cruel demands and their ungrateful attitudes, but all the same, bearing them seemed preferable to cooping myself up with knuckle-rapping holy sisters of whatever nationality for the rest of my life. My lack of enthusiasm for babies sometimes worried me, and I told my brother I thought I must be a faulty female because I lacked the maternal feelings that my mother assured me were the characteristic of all women, and with which she was so bountifully endowed. My brother, a year and a half younger, trying to be helpful, suggested I should give birth to a team of Brownies whom I could easily control with the toot of a whistle.

At that stage I accepted the inevitable. My brother was going to be a train driver, whereas I might marry one, become a nun or sit on the potty a lot and examine the results, and that was that.

Childhood had seemed permanent, but the fertile stage of my life seemed even more so. I settled down to giving over rather grudgingly to my womb, spacing my babies carefully so that I was never pregnant in the racing season and could continue to ride as a jockey. That there should be a stage beyond did not occur to me. Perhaps because no one mentioned its existence during my early years, now the menopause feels more temporary than the previous two phases.

During the years before the menopause I fretted because the possibility of having more children was running out, and I had no son. I have three daughters, and utterly adore them. The son would have been another thing altogether. The daughters are fun to be with, exciting to discuss things with, marvellous companions to share experiences with. Visiting their homes is being lapped in love and joyfulness. The son would probably have provided none of this; all the same, I wished for one.

My mother, in her eighties, hankered for a husband she

had grown old with. During the five years before the menopause, I felt like this about the son. I wanted one I had had all the time. As the deadline of the menopause approached, I planned visiting a specialist who could ensure me a male child, but apart from the fact that my husband did not want more children, the spectre of nappies, potties and babysitters all over again made my heart sink. In the end a lot of anguish and worrying took place that I admitted to no one, not even to my husband, Ranjit, but I did nothing at all about it. Any night I could have gone without contraception, yet I never did. I did not want a baby, I wanted a teenage son. Eventually the menopause put an end to all such hopes and, oddly, a stop to my ridiculous wishful thinking. At first the menopause felt like a signal of impending death. There seemed like an awfully short number of years left, and the days seemed to be passing at the most terrific speed. At one stage I got so concerned by the rushing days that I tried to make myself miserable to slow life down a bit.

I realized I had had my last period only in retrospect, unlike the other important changes of my life: being born, going to school, reaching puberty, making love, giving birth, getting my books published, and dying. You absolutely know that you are at school, or have got the curse for the first time, and the only reason you don't know you are dead is because you are dead.

After the onset of the menopause, with time for reflection because I was no longer busy with bringing up children, I began to anticipate a bleak future in which lost fertility was the least horrid aspect. A pain in the knee was surely the first twinge of rheumatism; forgetting where I had left the front door key heralded the onset of senile dementia. My swiftly approaching end seemed to offer no alternatives apart from extinction or – since I had been brought up as a Catholic – something rather worse.

My mother complained at this time that if you are travelling, you read a description of your destination and look on a map first, and it made her extremely cross to be expected to enter the land of death knowing nothing about it. 'I might not like it,' she wailed. 'I should be told.' I agreed. But worse even than what might be going to happen to me was the fear of losing beloved people and having a long and lonely old age. There did not seem at that stage to be anything that was even bearable, let alone pleasant, ahead.

Then I learned Transcendental Meditation, a technique for clearing the nervous system of a lifetime's accumulated stress, after which the individual, I was told, reaches her full potential and becomes supported by nature so that things go right for her. Now, instead of watching out for symptoms that gloomily point towards deterioration, I look out for positive and exciting ones heralding mental and physical improvement. One of these is when the mind starts to remain awake during sleep; another is witnessing, where a person witnesses her own body as though from another point of view. The best of all is experiencing happiness and being aware that even when things go wrong, the happy mood is still there, deep down.

I believe in the menopause in the way I used to believe in fairies as a child. It seems to me that the menopause, like magic, has its own form of subjective tangibility. Dogs don't have it, so why should I? Our Labrador had her womb removed, was prevented from jumping for three days, had her stitches out on the tenth day and was chasing rabbits on the eleventh. I have been told since that it is the upright position that causes human women to have such discomfort; the dog did not appear the least bit depressed, and had no hot flushes. As a child I had considerable contact with fairies who would answer my letters and requests, and on one occasion took my doll for a walk and returned her covered in mud with a bar of chocolate strapped to her hand with an elastic band. On a seaside holiday an older cousin helped me dig up a treasure trove buried by pirates. I thought I recognized the toffee tin that emerged, but my doubts were instantly banished when I opened it and found inside a halfpenny on which, appropriately, was the picture of a sailing boat. It was several years before I noticed that all halfpennies, even those which pirates had not buried a hundred years earlier, had this etched on them.

I felt bereft the day I discovered it was my mother who had done the tricks with the doll and the fairies, and my cousin who had buried the treasure. I regretfully came to terms with the fact that the whole thing was a hoax and there was no magic. After I learned TM I discovered that the magic was still there, that the other half of my body's life might be going to be even more productive than the first, and that I was not, after all, on a downhill-to-death run.

I began to suspect that the negative symptoms experienced by fifty-year-old women – depression, insomnia, drying up of sexual organs, loss of libido – were caused not by the menopause but by the stress of confronting an empty womb, a loss of purpose, inevitable physical and mental deterioration, and impending death. I was a dreadful pregnant woman, nauseous and cross, so when Ranjit realized that part of life was over he did not even try to conceal his delight. For us, with risks of pregnancy and the annoyance of contraceptives behind us, lovemaking, which was always beautiful, has been even better. Luckily, by the time I learned that sex after menopause is supposed to be uncomfortable or even impossible for most women, I already knew that it was not true for me.

A year after learning TM I did a further course called the 'siddhis', one aspect of which is yogic 'flying'. The preparation for this extraordinary experience is only rest. Once enough stress has been released from the body and its nervous system, one is able to have one's wishes fulfilled on a subtle level. I became able to make my body rise into the air by merely desiring it. On this course, as my body was being head-over-heeled and flung in its early toddling towards 'flying', I experienced my final period. I literally took off into the menopause, and it was an episode of hopefulness and optimism.

I hadn't liked games at school, and after I left I never played tennis or any other adult sport apart from race-riding in India. But after the onset of the menopause I began trying out various possibilities like yoga, jogging and swimming; and three years ago I added weight training. No one now said, 'Girls shouldn't lift weights.' At the gym, as my objective, I wrote that I wanted to be as fit when I was ninety as I was when I was twenty. A muscular nymphet solemnly keyed this into the gym computer, and came up with a programme of exercises and weight-lifting for me. I have felt tremendously encouraged by growing stronger and more flexible year after year at a time of life when women generally get less healthy and mobile.

I think a lot of menopausal problems come from the way other people think about women at that time. I felt fine at the gym until some young muscle-bound maiden reminded me, with a combination of contempt and admiration, that I am the oldest in the class by thirty years, adding: 'You are wonderful for your age.' And the advertisements I have been getting lately are for hearing aids and stair lifts: 'Now you have reached a time when you must be looking for ways to make your life easier.' On any morning I expect to find an advert urging me to purchase a set of incontinence pads.

A couple of years after learning to 'fly', Ranjit and I went to Holland for a meditation course lasting a month. We returned at one in the morning to find England under a glaze of brilliant February ice, and before we had even unlocked our front door we heard the thunder of water. Pipes had burst in a dozen places while we were away; water jetted out of the walls and through the ceilings in plaster-tinted torrents. The water was six inches deep on the floors, ceilings bulged, and great flanks of wallpaper flopped, dripping glue like the foliage of a tropical jungle. Lumps of wall plaster floated over the floors; attached to them by the nails I had hammered in were unrecognizable things that had once been pictures.

In that first horrified moment I saw how trivial and cosmetic house decor was. I suddenly understood that this decorating and colouring of a house's walls was a game, and as temporary as a stage set. Later, my inhibitions banished by the dimensions of the disaster, I let myself go on my rehabilitated walls, painting *trompe l'oeils* on them, sponging them, rag-rolling them, stencilling them, or hurling over them the same sort of carefree graffiti that had made us so cross with our poor little daughters years ago when they scribbled on the wallpaper. I felt as though I had been released from some kind of captivity as I rushed over every surface, slapping on emulsion and scrawling with pastels. I concentrated on the walls until they came to feel like some outer part of me, as though I was constructed like a set of Russian dolls, or walls-within-walls-within-walls, and the cosmos enclosing them all. Then the universe, the world, England, Oxford, our street, our house, my walls, my clothes, my body. It was like those long addresses I wrote for myself as a child: Sara Mostyn, Parsonage House, Stanton Harcourt, Oxon, England, the world, the universe, the cosmos. At the heart of the wall layers that made up me was the inner infinite eternal I had discovered during meditation. This thing was such a strong light that it could glow through all the other layers, transforming them if it was allowed to.

My taste in clothes has been affected by the menopause, for I no longer dress seeing myself as sexy or fertile, as I must subconsciously have done when I was those things. Nowadays I find that clothes are as fun and as trivial as wallpaper. I used to be very fat in my teenage years. Men thought me sexy then, which I did not like, and I have hated fatness ever since. I like to be skinny. Every man I have ever met, of every age and culture, seems perfectly dead certain that women want to look attractive to please them. I am equally certain that this is not the case with me. My husband grudgingly conceded: 'Oh well, perhaps you dress to impress other women, then.' This is not so either: I dress to please myself. I had proof that this was so the other day when the clothes I meant to wear were still wet. I put on something else and went next door to collect my mother's dog and take him for a walk. My brother, a renowned scrutinizer of female style, and two women, one young and one my own age, were there, and all three burst out in admiration: 'What gorgeous clothes! You do look nice. Are you going out somewhere?'

The dog and I passed a reflective window, and I saw myself. It was not what I liked. I was not what I wanted to be. I could not wait for my ninety-nine-pence black T-shirt, now hanging on the line, to be dry again.

For several years I dyed my hair, getting the biggest kick out of bright red, then wearing purple and orange to clash. I felt that my vibrant new locks were a big improvement on the mousey brown that nature had provided me with, but my daughters did not like it and begged me to 'Grow old gracefully, Mum', and in the end I gave in. I discovered that not only is grey hair a different colour, it's a different texture too – coarser and dryer. And it alters other people's view of you. In a *Guardian* interview I was described as 'grey-haired and stick thin'. This image did not appeal to me, nor fit in with my stylish idea of what I wanted to be.

The crunch came when I was travelling on the London Underground during the Gulf War. I was hanging on to a strap near the door in a packed compartment, waiting to get out at the next station. I was feeling fit and energetic, and planned to run up the stairs instead of taking the escalator when I got off because I needed the exercise. From the far end of the compartment an Arab began to signal to me to take his seat. There must have been a dozen women in the compartment as old or older than me, but because of my grey head he picked me out. As he nodded and bowed and waved, I decided he must be an Iraqi trying to ingratiate himself with the British public by offering up his seat to a grey-haired old lady. I shook my head, and tried to mouth back that I was getting out at the next station. He hopped up and down, imploring and begging me to avail myself of his courtesy. Everyone in the compartment started watching. The Arab became embarrassed, and his signalling became desperate. I began to feel beastly and ungrateful, and was even tempted to take his blinking seat and miss my station. But instead I leapt out like a rugger player when my stop came, and strode along the station with ostentatious vigour, hoping the Arab was looking and would realize his error. This episode made up my mind: I would go back to dyeing my hair – I decided that women who look unnecessarily old are not dignified but making a play for pity.

Several years ago I realized that I had sons after all without even knowing it. Ian, my eldest daughter's husband, is steady, kind and competent, and a marvellous father. Arild, Sabita's young Norwegian husband, is brilliantly clever, and as an expert with computers he has patiently helped me with mine. My youngest daughter, Juthika, and her husband, David, shared a house with us for seven years without conflict, though those must have been the years of the change. During that time, and ever since, David provided at least as much joy as the best of sons, and is vastly preferable to the worst.

My relationship with my daughters has altered over the years, though whether because of time or the menopause I do not know. I do not see them as my children now, but as marvellous and admirable people whose advice I value and whose company I enjoy. Sabita, my middle daughter, with her own business as an arts administrator, is the first person to read my manuscripts. When I need to make a moral decision I ask myself how Bijoya, a social worker and a patient and loving mother, would have handled it. Juthika is an adventurer, a traveller, and a meticulous business-woman – all things that I am not but wish I was. The fact that they originally had a nailhold in my womb's walls seems like a pleasant coincidence. Because I no longer need children, I do not feel the slightest need to weep for my lost womb – any more than I wept for my tonsils when they were taken out, or for my dummy after I had grown up.

I find my attitude towards men has changed, too. I was brought up with a brother who was younger, weaker and more delicate than me; throughout our childhood I adored, sheltered and protected him. I remember the first shock came when we were eight and nine, and he, not I, inherited my grandfather's gold watch 'because he was a boy'. As time passed, things like that happened thick and fast. I had to wash up, but he did not, 'because he was a boy'. Grown-ups were impressed by his kindness in talking to me as I waded through the family dishes. He went to a good school because boys, unlike girls, must have education. My brother was called the head of the family, although he was younger than me. The family property was entailed, so he inherited it all. He inherited the family title while I, through marriage, lost even the family name. I grew to accept these things as all women have to, and the first person ever to question them was my Indian mother-in-law.

'The boy getting everything is completely unfair,' she said firmly. 'In India property is divided equally between all the children.' Resentment, however, did not properly awaken in me till the menopause, as though only then was the female part of me discarded and I felt as worthy of manhood as my brother, though of course I was still not offered it. This resentment, which I regretted and disliked but was unable to banish, became transferred to all patronizing men, like masters of ceremony at banquets who toast 'the lovely ladies who grace this occasion' as though the women guests were nicely starched napkins; weddings where men make all the speeches and 'give away' a girl wrapped in white like a parcel; men whose attitude comes out like 'Ranjit has left his shoes, his socks and his wife in the hall.' Ranjit, I must add, is not at all this sort of man. He admires and respects women for what they think and do as well as what they are and look like, and he dislikes them being patronized as much as I do.

The human race has come a long way since the first amoeba, and is still evolving and metamorphosing, becoming more intelligent and skilful all the time. Human women are the only creatures who go on living for a long time after they have ceased to be reproductive, and I believe that this is because for the second half of their lives they are designed to fulfil a second purpose. As the eyes are for crying and looking, the mouth is for talking and eating, the nose is for smelling and breathing, so perhaps a woman's reproductive system has a second use as well, of which we are not yet properly aware. Men remain fertile more or less to the end of their lives, yet women stop being so when they are strong and healthy in all other ways. There must be some good evolutionary reason for this, and I think it is connected with a grand human destiny. Perhaps it is because we have had to give up half our evolutionary lives to attracting men, and bearing and bringing up children, that we women are being allowed a second half to evolve spiritually. Before the menopause we had to keep ourselves looking pretty, otherwise men would not love us. We had to keep ourselves strong, otherwise we would not be able to bear children. We had to keep ourselves flexible for bringing up children. But after the menopause we are still capable of all these things, since we have already practised them.

So far I have always been protected and hemmed in by walls. What I am hoping for next, now that the womb walls have become still, is that I will learn to live without the other walls that surround me, protect me, hem me in. I have had several changes already, and would like to keep on changing until I have shed my reliance on walls completely. I have already taken up windows, for you can't see Infinity through the walls, and those walls that were so important when the children were growing up and needed to be kept safe from danger, from the weather, and from seeing too far into the future in case they noticed bleakness there, have no place in my life now. I have painted all the house walls white, taken out the nails, filled the holes and put away the pictures, and I have had all the windows repaired and cleaned.

When I began to write this I told Ranjit I was grateful to him for still loving me even though I was no longer a wench. He said, 'You were never a wench to me. You were Sara, you are Sara, and you will always be Sara.' I want to have those windows so clean that I can see myself through them and recognize the truth of Ranjit's statement: that though I am always changing, the change itself has not really changed me, because there is always one permanent aspect to me. I am.

'IF IT AIN'T BROKE, DON'T FIX IT'

Deirdre Bair

On a fine summer day in 1974, when I was thirty-nine, I realized with great trepidation that my period was one day late. I am not a hypochondriac, nor was I hysterical; it was a truly alarming situation, because from my first menstruation at the age of thirteen, my periods had been so regular that I knew almost to the hour when they would begin. In fact, although I have been a lapsed Catholic since the age of ten, my husband and I joked about the scrupulous Catholicity of the only form of birth control we found necessary: rhythm, which alerted us to when we should use condoms. My cycle was so predictable that I had only to say, 'This month I want to become pregant,' and that is how each of my children was conceived. With a history such as this, a period one day late was cause for terrible anxiety, especially as I was on the threshold of many different kinds of change.

Several years earlier, I had left a developing career as a

literary journalist to pursue a doctorate in comparative literature. In 1974 I was deep into the research that resulted in the biography of Samuel Beckett, and I was about to begin a university teaching career. Also, my children were in their late teens and embarking on their university studies, and my husband and I were frankly looking forward to daily life without them. The last thing in the world I wanted in 1974 was another pregnancy.

I waited a week, then went to the doctor. 'You're not pregnant,' he said, 'you're just late.'

No, I insisted. I am not late, because if I were, something else had to be terribly wrong. As far as he was concerned, I was late and that was it. The doctor's eyes never met mine, but darted instead around the small consulting room as if he were plotting how to escape from this embarrassingly crazy woman. I could sense how much he wanted to get away from me and on to his next (and possibly more compliant) patient, so in a fit of perversity, I went slowly and carefully into all the details of my menstrual history. I tried to explain – patiently, I thought – that, without fail, one month my cycle was twenty-three days, the next twenty-seven. The long cycle came and went without incident. The short cycle brought some discomfort: my breasts were tender for several days, and I usually had some twinges in the lower back. However, none of it was enough to incapacitate me and I could not truthfully say that it was painful. Occasionally I felt chilly, but a brief nap under a warm coverlet usually made me feel better. In both cycles, the periods themselves were regular: about three to four days in duration.

At that point I made the mistake of pausing for breath. 'Well, you're not pregnant,' the doctor boomed, stabbed my chart emphatically with his pen, and bounded out of the room. As I was leaving the building, I bumped into him in the narrow hallway of his consulting area, and as an afterthought, this doctor (whom I never saw again after this visit) called me into his private office. He was as offhand and disinterested in the conversation that followed as he had been earlier in the consulting room. I don't remember being upset at the time, but recalling his attitude today makes me furious.

'You just might be starting the menopause,' he said. 'And if you begin to miss a period now and again this early in life, it's going to be difficult. I guess I should put you on oestrogen.'

I must say that I had no idea what he was talking about. I certainly knew that menopause meant the cessation of menstruation and the end of fertility, but that is truly all I knew of it in 1974. I knew no one who had even had the menopause, which will not be so surprising once I describe my family history. As for oestrogen, it was the first time I had ever heard the word. So I asked a few simple questions about it, and got no satisfactory answers.

He did warn me, however, in what was little more than a mumble, that 'Oh, by the way, there may or may not be' what he called 'some sort of link' between oestrogen therapy and an increased risk of 'either breast or cervical cancer. But we really don't know yet.' I was both astonished and alarmed at his casual diagnosis of menopause and cavalier attitude towards the possibility of cancer. 'Well, if it ain't broke, don't fix it,' I replied. I declined oestrogen therapy and left, never to return.

The curious thing is: had he not been so indefinite in offering unspecific doses of possibly experimental drug therapy, if he had instead said firmly, 'You *must* take XX number of pills YY times daily,' I probably would have done so, for those were the years in which I (and most of the women I knew) would not have dreamed of questioning a physician. I think what saved me here was that I grew up in a household where the most significant medications were

Vicks salve, Vaseline, generic aspirin and witch hazel. I realize now how fortunate my brother, my sister and I were to be born with glorious good health, but our family's attitude was that anything else was simply not permitted, and that probably had something to do with how we treated our bodies and expected them to behave. So to commit myself to a lifetime of popping a random sampling of pills because I had missed one period was unthinkable.

That evening, I spoke to my mother, and for the first time in my life we talked about the possibility of menopause. 'You are not unusual,' she said. 'You are right on target.' She, her mother and her three sisters all had the menopause between the ages of thirty-seven and thirty-nine. Their periods simply stopped, they never had a hot flash (the first time I heard this expression), and never took a single pill. All had strong bones and good teeth, and lived remarkably long lives. None ever had anything more than what my mother called 'the usual moodiness, caused by real life and not hormones'. Furthermore, she added, my father's mother and his only sister had had exactly the same experience, so my paternal heritage paralleled the maternal. 'Just go on doing what you're doing,' was my mother's advice. 'It won't bother you if you don't let it.'

I can't describe the sense of freedom and elation I felt in the first few years after I stopped menstruating. If menstruation had caused me any problem or discomfort at all, it had been work-related and of a very practical nature. I was a newspaper reporter during most of my adult reproductive years, and it was inevitable that during my period, my editor (a man) would send me on an assignment which required a 'stake-out', i.e. standing outside an office building far into the night, or sitting in a car somewhere along a deserted country road waiting to take a statement from someone coming out of a house or a motel or a meeting. Finding the privacy to change sanitary supplies had been one of my two main concerns; the other was finding a purse big enough to carry all the bulky equipment I needed. And when I began to do the travelling required for research before I could write the biography of Beckett, it was even more of a hassle. I never knew to what small Irish country town or French village an interview or an archive would call me, so I had to be prepared because of doubts about what supplies the local stores would have on hand. Bulky pads and tampons took up so much room in the luggage that I can distinctly remember my exhilaration when I saw how many boxes of tape cassettes or how big a pile of books I could fit into the space they formerly occupied.

I know I did not think about the fact that I had breezed through the menopause, for the simple reason that I assumed all women went through it as easily as I had done. I never discussed it until recently, and then only because my friends have begun to experience it in degrees ranging from discomfort to pain. I don't have anything to contribute to these conversations except to say that mine was long ago over, and oh boy, am I glad of it. Yet somehow, I am embarrassed to say even that, because I know no one whose experience is similar to mine. I am not imagining this, but when I do tell my story, most of my friends look at me as if something is wrong with me. So I try not to say anything. Indeed, when the editor of this volume asked me to contribute, I declined at first because, as I wrote to her, 'I don't have anything to say.' That was exactly the point, she argued, persuading me to write.

In the intervening years, every single doctor I consulted seemed puzzled by my family history and the ease with which we women dispensed with what others found troublesome and frequently traumatic. I consulted four gynaecologists after the original one because I lived in several different cities in the 1980s. All except one were women, but all were equally concerned. They listened thoughtfully, took careful histories, then sent me off for every kind of testing, from blood to bone. All seemed amazed to find that – to use a layperson's language – my bones were solid and dense, my hormones were in the correct range, and my skin was as supple as that of a woman ten years younger. They all agreed that I had no need of immediate hormone replacement therapy, but each doctor independently recommended that I begin it anyway. To each I replied with what had by now become my favourite maxim: 'If it ain't broke, don't fix it.'

I take this position because each year that I have a smear and mammogram, I am told there has been no negative change in the condition of my body. So I have yet to begin any kind of medication, despite the usual recommendation that I should do so as a precautionary measure. I listen to what each doctor says, and I understand that they have opted for a 'preventive first strike' (to use one of their favourite analogies, all of which are curiously combative and warlike). But I respectfully decline because I just can't see myself beginning a lifelong regimen of medication until it is necessary.

Nevertheless, menopause is much on my mind these days. Many of my friends are literally suffering through it, their lives disrupted by bodies that are suddenly betraying them. At times I pale before their anger and rage. Others feel moderate forms of discomfort, and still others are traumatized because of how they fear their immediate society will regard them once they are no longer fertile. It is sad for me to see several friends, women of achievement and accomplishment in so many aspects of their lives, who are severely depressed because they can no longer become pregnant. 'Call me irrational, I don't care,' says one, a beautiful, vibrant woman of fifty-five, as she invokes a litany of imagined changes that she swears have turned her into a 'hag, crone, witch' – her words, certainly not mine.

Perhaps it was easier for me both mentally and physically because of my personal situation when it happened. I had – and still have – a passionate marriage. I had already given birth to all the children I wanted, so I had nothing to prove in that quarter, either to myself or to others. I had a stimulating intellectual life and a career that brought me respect as well as satisfaction. I have a large extended family and many sustaining friendships, and I wish I had more time to give to all of them. For me, menopause was not the end of anything but, rather, the glorious beginning of freedom. I could work and travel unencumbered, and I was marvellously liberated from fear of unwanted pregnancy.

While I was writing this piece, I thought back to myself as I was in those years when women, having discovered that they could be or do anything, believed they had to do it all. I myself thought I had to be the perfect wife, mother, hostess, housekeeper, volunteer, and professional woman. In retrospect, I think the menopause was the catalyst that helped me to focus my energies on the areas in which I wanted satisfaction. It made me realize that time was evaporating, and I had to concentrate on those aspects of my life that mattered most. I wanted to succeed in my personal relationships, and I wanted to be respected professionally (the two qualities that eventually led me to write the biography of Simone de Beauvoir, partly to help me understand my own choices in life). I stopped trying to do, or be, all things to all people.

My personal experience helped me, too, in terms of my professional life. In the past ten years, I have studied the way women's lives have been shaped by the culture and society in which they live and, conversely, how women, through their daily life and work, have effected change in both. When I wrote about Simone de Beauvoir, I had an immediate, instinctive understanding of how she had been able to live life so fully, how she had been so prolific in her writing. She and I both believed the major reason for this was that she had been liberated from the tyranny of her body's demands because they had been so few. Like mine, her menstruation was regular and did not interfere with her work. Menopause for her also 'just happened one day and that was that'. I remember a conversation we had about this, both of us amazed to find at last another woman with a similar experience. We talked at length, wondering why it had been so easy for us and so difficult for everyone else we knew.

We differed, however, when I expressed genuine sympathy for women who mourned or feared the end of fertility. For Simone de Beauvoir, these women were 'being silly'. I interpreted her remark more kindly than it seems at first glance. I asked if she felt this way because work was always the most important aspect of her life, and bearing children had never been something she wanted.

'Yes,' she said. 'If only women could get beyond that attitude they have about men and children, if they could turn their thoughts elsewhere, then they would not suffer as they do.' Perhaps, I thought, unable in this instance, as in so many others, to agree with her. I turned the conversation to another topic, because I knew that we had come to an unresolvable impasse in our thinking.

Now I am writing about Anaïs Nin, and that is quite another matter. I am glad that menopausal women are now 'out' of a different kind of 'closet', and that other women have given me so much information to help me understand her. Nin's menopause was late, and its onset coincided with the publication of her Diaries when she was in her early sixties. Ironically, all her life she had craved fame, and when it finally came, she was too ill to enjoy it. She spent the last decade of her life battling first a cruel menopause and then the cancer that killed her.

Hers was a horrible death, which she recorded in every

ghastly detail in an unpublished diary called *The Book of Pain*. She willingly endured every indignity because life meant so much to her and she was determined to beat the odds. Her illness was first diagnosed as a pre-cancerous cervix, and spread rapidly from there. Disfiguring surgery and several courses of radiation treatment led to chemo-therapy and vaginal cobalt insertions. When these failed, she turned to homeopathy, spiritualism, faith healers and magic.

But before this, she had one of the most difficult passages through menopause I have ever encountered. Writing about Anaïs Nin, I have been truly humbled before her devastat-ing experience. At the height of her great fame, in the onslaught of publicity that followed publication of the Diaries, she withdrew from time to time into various hospitals for repeated surgery to stop the heavy bleeding. Eventually, she had a hysterectomy. This was followed by hormone therapy, which did not succeed in controlling the deep depression that reduced this active, dynamic woman to catatonic inertia. For the better part of her last decade she was in and out of hospitals, seeking out every sort of therapy – from those at the forefront of medical research to those best described as sheer quackery. As I read her own vivid accounts of her suffering, I cannot help but shudder in gratitude that my experience was so different.

Today, there is much open discussion of what, only a short time ago, was an unmentionable topic. Books and articles proliferate. Physicians and research scientists argue over varying methodologies; analysts offer a broad spectrum of treatment, from behaviour modification to drug therapy; women share histories, remedies, and even bibliographies. From all of the above, I have learned (among much else) that my experience represents either 10 or 15 per cent of the total menopausal population of the United States and Great

Britain. (I have been unable to determine if this statistic applies elsewhere, but a recent study of menstruating women in such diverse cultures as the United States, Italy and Bahrain has found that although they call it by different names, all exhibit the same symptoms of pre-menstrual syndrome. Perhaps a study of menopausal women would find similar results.)

I wonder about the statistic that says I represent such a small percentage of the total population of post-menopausal women. If it is true, should not I and others like me be the subject of medical research, carried out for the benefit of the other 85–90 per cent of the female population? If it is false, if there is a larger percentage of women whose experience mirrors mine, why is this fact so hidden? Certainly, suffering is always more dramatic and colourful; hot flashes and temper tantrums do make better press than business as usual. But shouldn't women be offered the histories of those who do not suffer, so that this possibility might at least be held out to them? Shouldn't they be told that there are women who pass through this cycle of life without incident? One of my friends, who shared her experiences specifically for this piece, suddenly blurted out, 'Good God, can it be that I have these occasional hot flashes because I am expected to have them, not because they are real?' Is she on to something here: do all the stories of women's suffering promote psychosomatic manifestations that become real because no other alternative is offered to them? Where do the answers lie?

Probably in research. I am delighted to read that government agencies and private groups have begun to question the paucity of research that has been done on women. I rejoice when physicians say they are now considering establishing a speciality in women's specific health needs.

And probably, also, answers lie in bringing our experiences out into the open. Books such as this collection of diverse testimonies do much to further discussion among women. I am reluctant to use the current buzz word 'empowerment', but this is exactly what women must do. They must arm themselves with the most and the best information so that they can make the wisest choices for themselves as they pass through what should not be the end of all positive living, but just another cycle in a woman's glorious existence.

'MUCH THANKS'
Phyllida Law

I did not enjoy having the curse. It began when a strange dull stain appeared in what were known as my 'knicker linings', a stout pair of cotton garments worn under navy-blue bloomers. I hid them under the wardrobe and resigned myself to Death. I don't remember pain. Just fear and a dignified acceptance of an inevitable fate. I was eleven years old, and there was a war on.

When the knicker deficit became severe, I had to confess. Wordless and terrified, I was put to bed in my mother's room with a hot-water bottle. I remember her brushing her hair at the dressing-table and sighing heavily in a knowing sort of way, implying that I was in for something now which included pain, emotional trauma, and MEN. My Aunt May stuck her head round the door and, with a burst of cleansing laughter, invited me to join some sort of club. I was consulted on what I might like to eat for tea in case I felt 'seedy', and Aunt May and Mother discussed degrees of pain and discomfort. I felt neither. Apparently, however, I had some sort of illness which every woman had and, though unpleasant, it was not terminal – it would only try and kill me once a month. In view of my undisclosed conviction that I had been dying, this was quite good news.

A bulky package was brought to my bedside later in the day which included some surgically pink cross-gartering for the stomach and a daintily looped gauze-covered cushion for the crutch. We had a rehearsal before the gas fire. The puzzling little belt gave no hint of the indecent tangle of perished grey elastic which lurked in the sponge bags of my life.

It was wartime. I had been evacuated at the age of seven, and now attended, as the only boarder, a small school on the Clyde. At the end of the holidays I was dispatched there as usual in the corner of the train's Ladies Only compartment. The new apparatus took up a lot of space in my small suitcase. Miss Jennie and Miss Meg must have been informed that, having had lice the previous term, I now had my monthly period. And that was that.

Nothing more happened.

It was a false alarm.

The great sex therapist Chad Varah started the Samaritans after officiating at the funeral of a child who committed suicide when she discovered she had started 'to bleed between her legs'. That was in 1935 when, as he puts it, 'No adult ever gave a child a straight answer.'

He had a Puritan background. So did my mother. She was the daughter of a Presbyterian minister in Glasgow. My grannie had eight children, five of whom were daughters, and she used to ration their sanitary towels, handing them out from a locked cupboard, one by one, on request. The only advice she ever gave the girls (including my mother) when they became engaged to be married was to buy nightgowns that buttoned down the front.

Back at school, I started private research. My mother had been evasive. Maybe I asked no questions, but she was probably unnerved by acquiring an eleven-year-old woman, and her unhappiness with my father, whom she was soon to divorce, gave her an air of bitterness and regret which made her seem unapproachable. Like Héloïse discovering she was pregnant by reading Aristotle, I hoped to find some hard facts in the books that lined the schoolroom walls. I drew a complete blank with Scott and Dickens, whose heroines appalled me. George Eliot fitted my mood. I liked 'him'. Maggie Tulliver was my hero. She had a satisfactorily tragic life and died young, a fate I seemed anxious to follow.

I came across the chilly word 'menstruation' in a luridly illustrated encyclopaedia which I read avidly and which, combined with wartime posters in public lavatories, persuaded me that I had VD. Amongst the symptoms listed were a white discharge and spots on or near the genitalia. The onset of puberty produces the first in women. I don't know why I had an ulcer on my bum.

Aunt May, whose general merriment made her easier to question than most, said that the large posters in the street meant Digging for Victory, but I had collected enough false information to know that what I had was Rude and a disease that drove you to madness and early death.

My friend Isobel Hebblethwaite confirmed my diagnosis, and said I had caught it from a loo seat. When I stayed with her I peed in the sink and determined to devote my short life to humanity and become a doctor.

In that summer holiday – or perhaps even the next, for there seemed to be a very long intermission – my brother and I went to Skye, and waking on our first morning to peerless white sands and blue skies, I knelt at the window to gaze. My brother woke and shouted. My bed was full of blood. I felt nothing but shame, obscurely comforted by my brother's brisk efficiency and by the landlady's daughter, who changed my sheets as if it were a matter of course.

On the phone my mother said a change of climate and good sea air often 'brought you on', and not to get constipated. The curse had come upon me. My friend Isobel said I would die if I had a bath. I got pulsating spots on my chin, my back was solid with acne, and you had to buy sanitary towels from men in chemists.

How did St Joan manage? All that armour. How did Pavlova, when she danced *Swan Lake* in that plate-like tutu? Who invented tampons? Have they been knighted?

I was sent to a skin specialist with a terribly pockmarked face who prescribed a sun ray lamp and said I would be cured when I was thirty. I supposed he meant *sex*. I supposed people generally had that when they were thirty.

When I was thirteen I was sent to an impressive English boarding school where there was a girl who still had her prisoner-of-war number tattooed on her arm. She wore two sanitary towels and used the swimming pool. I discovered hockey was a help. I grew unlikely breasts like the ones I had seen in the *National Geographic* magazine, and at half-term my mother, wearing an alarming hat, handed me a Kestos bra in the school corridor. I had joined the Club and settled down to thirty-nine of what they call childbearing years.

My two daughters are well into theirs. They are enviably offhand about pushing objects up the important orifice known to them as 'the front bum'. They are also devastatingly open about it, whereas the pressure on young women of my generation to stay silent was strong, and came from unexpected sources. I was very young when I read Elizabeth Goudge's *Green Dolphin Country*. In it a male character says something to the effect that 'Women always make a fuss about the inevitable.' I remember wondering if my father had left my mother because of such behaviour, and became a Stoic on the spot.

Much later I read, in the lightly censored newspapers placed every day in our school hall, that it was considered inadvisable for a woman to drive a car when she was menstruating, or for her ever to be a JP, as her judgement would be impaired one week in every month. I simply arranged to behave as if I never menstruated in case I was prevented from becoming a doctor.

Stories had already reached me from Glasgow's distinguished medical faculty that there was a particular professor who disapproved of female students. In order to display their unsuitability, he would ask them to stand up in what were then male-dominated lecture rooms and watch sardonically as he requested details of penile erections or vaginal discharge. This last tiresome symptom still persuaded me on gloomy days that I had VD. I didn't tell my mother till I was seventeen. I had reached university, and I was wretched. Misery can be creative, and it became clear to me that I was absolutely in the wrong place.

I asked my mother if I might give up the idea of medicine, and her easy response so unnerved me that I broke down and told her that in any case I would not live long, and that I had venereal disease. She told me that I hadn't. The doctor diagnosed anaemia. I was prescribed iron pills. Mother was wise about ignorance and fear.

I sprang like released elastic back to my instinctive gifts, and went to drama school. Nobody ever told my grandmother. Theatre was the work of the Devil.

Apparently I told my daughters that I went into the theatre because you could go up to any man, be he knight or understudy, and ask for directions to the Ladies' Lavatory, whereupon you would receive helpful and possibly even accurate directions without a stammer or a blush. It is true that I was offended by male attitudes of the day in Scotland. There was a distinctly men-only zone in conversation and social life, which needed more courage and wit to broach than I possessed. I hated the bursts of laughter in corners broken up in sniggering disarray when a 'lady' appeared. I learned to enjoy dirty stories only when they were coeducational.

I was mortified that my presence was so disturbing to people I wanted to know. Was it my fault? The rosy-faced, snowy-haired church officer who was kind to us on school church outings met me in my summer frock and my first Ponds lipstick, and gave me a French kiss. Distinguished middle-aged men courted and admired by my elders did much the same. 'Don't be ridiculous, Phyllida, he was just trying to be nice.'

I learned to avoid men wearing raincoats or carrying them, spent a long train journey in the guard's van, and an even longer one on the luggage rack of an Italian train. Travelling in Catholic countries was torture. Did the Pope know?

But these shrivelling encounters of my early youth were cauterized by laughter and a joyous time at theatre school. Much red tape was cut. Shakespeare was unexpurgated, and we struggled with our sexuality together.

Imagine being the son of a coal miner in the early 1950s and having to appear in a jockstrap and tights for morning exercises to the strains of the 'Skater's Waltz'. My digs were in a ballet school, where drying jockstraps jostled bras and diverse gussets on the washing line, and the Christmas tree one year was decorated with white kitchen candles and little fluffy tampons. The lid blew off my life, and everything was all right. Like falling in love.

I married an actor. We shrieked over birth control. At first we sent away for a little black box advertised in the *New Statesman*. Properly programmed with the dates of your monthly period, it would register the only days in the month for 'safe sex', a phrase that has rather a different connotation nowadays. We left it behind one holiday.

So we had Emma.

There were other ingenious devices on offer which I first read about in Mary McCarthy's *The Group*: a book that caused, I remember, grave offence among men.

There was this copper coil. Implanted. I thought it sounded medieval, like a chastity belt, and no doubt it will appear so to future generations. So I settled for a Dutch cap: an intriguingly sprung little item liberally decorated with spermicidal cream which, when squeezed for insertion, shot like a flying saucer about the loo and lodged itself on the lampshade.

I inserted it upside-down for a week. My weary instructress at the local clinic said, 'You might as well have worn it in your ear, Mrs Thompson.' My gynaecologist (the late Helena Wright) would look over her specs and say, 'It is not an emotional decision to insert a Dutch cap.' So I wore it almost permanently. On my yearly visits Helena would open the little plastic box where it lay scrubbed for the occasion and say, 'Well, it's a triumph, Mrs Thompson,' before throwing it into the waste-paper basket.

And then there was Sophie.

I once heard a woman at a health farm saying, in patrician tones, 'I can't think why we don't just lay an egg and keep it in the airing cupboard.' But if you become pregnant it tends to be good news. There is a baby at the end of it.

The menopause has no such joyful ring, and it appears to lead nowhere but down. 'I've got the menopause,' would be difficult to say on a trampoline. It's difficult to say at all. It ranks high on the list of words you wouldn't want to say in Bible class: 'Menstruation, Masturbation, Menopause.'

Horrible.

If you tell an acquaintance who wishes to borrow a tampon

that you no longer keep them in the house she becomes instantly respectful, as if you have a life-threatening disease. If you say you have a bus pass, much the same happens. There is no doubt it has everything to do with Age, for how can anyone mourn the passing of all that plugging and pushing and assorted inconvenience? Could not we think of the menopause as simply a form of effective birth control? It means you can't have babies. It most emphatically does not mean the end of your sex life. What an offensive idea. Hands up those of us who last had sex purely for procreational purposes.

I last had sex ten years ago: three days before I was widowed. Our daughters were grown up, and babies had nothing to do with it. I was fifty. I never had the curse again. My womb simply retired, without further symptoms or side-effects.

Did my libido take the same cue? I don't believe it did. I think my new freedom would have inspired my husband and me. We were like kids when we had the house to ourselves. Human sexuality varies from red to white, with every shade of pink in between, and I don't know where we came on this Richter scale, but I suspect we were both terminally monogamous.

New widows are very vulnerable. Even standing in the queue at the post office I would have to prevent myself from leaning my face against the male shoulders in front of me, if only to breathe male warmth through wet tweed. But how could I be unfaithful to someone who seemed only to have gone on an extended tour overseas? Besides, no one offered.

My daughters sat on the edge of my bath the other day and commented on how my 'boobs' were much improved, and said that I should 'take a lover'. From where? Who? A friend who came to my bachelor flat recently looked at my bedroom and said, 'This is the bedroom of a racy nun.' My signalling system may have packed up with my womb. Shock and bereavement played their part, I am sure, but rumour had it that the menopause makes itself felt in any number of uncomfortable ways, so I did a bit of local research.

I asked my eighty-year-old mother if she remembered the menopause.

'Well, it was a long time ago,' she said doubtfully.

'I know, but how was it?'

'A perfect nuisance.'

I asked for details.

'Well, I was rushing about at Domestic Science College . . .'

'No, darling, that's when you had your monthly period. I mean the menopause.'

'The what?'

'The change of life.'

'Oh, *that*,' she said dismissively. 'Never noticed it.'

Perhaps this piece of luck is hereditary?

As far as I was concerned, I was suddenly single-celled. My body was handed back to me. Free. And so was a slice of leftover life. I did a lot of clearing up, I remember. And cleaning. Rather like when one is about to give birth.

I had a new job appearing in the West End in Michael Frayn's farce *Noises Off*.

I moved house and created my own flat and my own garden. Sitting in the sun one evening, I said to Emma, who was in the tiny kitchen, 'What a lovely view it is looking from the garden through the sitting-room and seeing you in the kitchen.'

'Has it not occurred to you, Mother,' she said, 'that you created the view entirely by yourself?'

Nearly.

It was a complete 'change of life'.

But you see, for most women who suffer the menopause – and I am told 50 per cent of us do suffer – there is nothing.

There is no drama in this private, unpublicized event. No new job. Not much sympathy, and certainly not the powerful support from friends, family and colleagues such as I had when my husband died.

No change of life. It's what doctors tend to call a 'natural-function-don't-fuss-next-please' situation.

I believe a subterranean energy and power is released at the menopause, but we must be able to plug it in somewhere, or it is stifled. It can become a negative charge. A blockage.

I remember watching Margaret Thatcher growing more radiant by the day when she became Prime Minister. People tell me it's HRT. Well, perhaps. I think it is confidence, success and power. And a greatly improved wardrobe. Money. We're back to Virginia Woolf again. A womb of one's own.

If I were Prime Minister I would be assassinated within the week, but I would hope to get Tampax on the NHS and a grant for women on the occasion of the change of life in the hope that it could. A tidy sum. Let's not call it a lump sum. There would be significant debriefing with the therapist of your choice and a lot of champagne to celebrate sheer self-interest.

So here I am on the vast plateau of middle age. Late middle age. A Queen Mother, reviewing a decade of chaste independence and the muddled history of my womanhood, childhood, puberty, childbearing, menopause and post-menopause, whatever that is. Five stages compared to Shakespeare's seven ages of man, and rather more mewling and puking.

What can I say to my daughters about my 'strange, eventful history'? Thank you, my darlings, for your continuing support as founder members of the West Hampstead

Women's Support Group. You have reached your child-bearing years with enviable flamboyance and a lot more information than I had. You are both established in our profession in ways far beyond my sketchy attempts at a career.

You may not be able to pee standing up, an enviable accomplishment, but you have tasted intoxicating freedoms, and I hope you are hooked. Your father admired boldness, originality and freestanding furniture. I am not concerned here just with an improved strain in the erratic progress of female emancipation. I wanted you to acquire a real sense of yourselves so that you might take a proper control over your own developing powers before anyone else did.

You know how much I have approved when my twentieth-century daughters, with their twentieth-century sex lives, have lived alone, whether for three months or three years. What a privilege it is, this room of one's own. It can be frightening. It is exhilarating. It gives you priceless self-confidence. Remember it. It will be yours again. How can a woman who has never known this sort of freedom recognize it as such in her menopausal years, and use it as her right? If society tells you at the menopause that it is the end of your 'useful' life, I hope you will tell society it is an ass.

My grandmother was bored by women. 'Females' she called them. She wanted only sons, because they had passports to a party from which she was largely excluded. I am glad I escaped into the theatre, where the equality of the sexes must be one of my chief delights in life.

Another is the equality of the ages backstage. We seem absolutely equal under the skin, whether wrinkled or smooth. From 'out front', things look sadly different. The pressures on you to be for ever young, slim, beautiful, and never to admit to the menopause, are much greater than ever I endured. At the end of the war, youth did not exist as a commercial commodity. Television and teenagers were not invented. We wore our mothers' clothes and longed to be thirty.

Advertising was charmingly retrograde. Azora Hair Cream for men. Virol: anaemic girls need it. I had it. If your husband looked tired, you were urged to buy Horlicks for 'night starvation', and if *you* looked tired he urged you to buy Ponds Cold Cream. American Fulbright Scholars gave us an early glimpse of *Dallas* with Coca Cola, and exquisitely engineered underwear which seemed to be made of spun sugar. Ours was boilable.

But we were idealists, scornful of glamour and the West End. French windows and matinée idols were 'out', kitchen sinks were 'in', and even if we weren't, we looked to a steady progression of roles in the classic repertory system which would give us the confidence and faith in our talent to transcend whatever looks we had.

Beauty can be acted. I've seen it done superbly. Think of Lynn Fontanne, who said, 'I've got a bottom like a pear and I have found thirteen positions in which my bottom does not appear like a pear. Those are my thirteen positions.' Or think of Edith Evans, who practised 'positive affirmation' in front of her dressing-room mirror: 'I am beautiful,' she said. And she was. It's not so easy on the screen, perhaps, especially in close-up, and the repertory system no longer operates as it did, which doesn't help our training.

I watch you both refusing to be impaled on this pickle-fork and admire your creative disdain. You have so much more confidence than I had. Mine was stunted by being an 'evacuee'. At seven years old I found myself unwanted. A nuisance who caught fleas, didn't know who Adam and Eve were, and had her hat elastic snapped to make her eyes water. I know I am a damaged creature.

What interests me and may amuse you is that I think I

am damaged in precisely the way that many men are who were sent away at a tender age and brought up entirely amongst their own sex. I always felt that the public-school system operated against women. When I started acting, directors tended to emerge from that world, and they had a very limited view of the 'fair sex'. It helped to go blonde. But when it came to boarding-school girls like me, no wonder they went to Sweden to cast their ideal women. I looked like Matron. A hefty girl; no one knew what to do with me. In my twenties I played ancient creatures in padding, dyed blankets and far too much make-up. I became adept at making false noses out of Copydex, and I even played the back end of a cow. Julian Slade called me the 'udder half'. Longing to be someone else, I was always a character actress, so I have a certain durability. Middle age is an asset.

I did not have great beauty, so I don't miss it, and though I admired it, I have never greatly envied it. I think it's a bit of a stumbler for a girl. A beauty born up to advertising standards will be in trouble well before the menopause. You two, in any case, were busy showing the world you were not 'just pretty faces' and putting a moustache on the *Mona Lisa*. The past was not to be all-powerful. You were going to find your own way forward.

Absolutely.

In my day, we sat about complaining that parts weren't written for us. Your generation has begun to write them. Now we complain that there are no major roles written for 'older' women, menopausal women. We will have to write them. Books are getting bolder.

Mary Wesley didn't get published till she was seventy, and she regularly offends by her blunt talk about sex. This is because of her age. People think she either doesn't or shouldn't know about such matters. There is nothing for it – we must become more vociferous and visible.

I heard a woman on the radio the other day saying, 'We need more grannies on the streets.' We also need them on the stage. We must exit disgracefully. And another thing: I had actually believed that the 'permissive age' had improved things to the extent that men no longer exposed themselves in mid-afternoon in Merton Park. Wrong. They do not expose themselves to *me*. My age protects me from other such unpleasantnesses. Out of respect for it, people will stop telling me disturbing facts or talking to me about important things. Whisperingly excluded from real life in my youth, I refuse to be marginalized and remaindered simply because I neither menstruate nor fuck. Please call in with disgraceful gossip. Nothing bland.

Please don't allow me to retire. I need the money. I need it to go to the Galapagos. I need it to fund the adventures you will write about. I need to escape, if only now and then, from the classic trap that snaps at the ankles of menopausal women. The bank manager expected me to retire to Scotland when I was widowed. I doubt if he ever noticed that I worked. He thought I would manage quite nicely if I went North. Just about. He knew I had elderly parents. Society had found a 'carer'. It is expected of me. I had finished nursing my mother-in-law, my brother and my husband, my children were grown up. I am a widow. A woman. A daughter. What else should I do? Society will give me an 'attendance allowance' which will get me once round Sainsbury's. Society is a pig. I'll do it, and I'll enjoy it if it kills me, but please don't let me retire.

Look what happens to men. They get 'distressing physical symptoms' and 'violent swings of mood'. My stepfather wanted to commit suicide. It's tough, but I'll take my vitamins if you'll take yours. Your profession – I'm sorry, I mean *our* profession – lays a heavy burden on you, which is that you must always be well. Because of this you will have to listen to your body, and respond to it with steady good sense. The show must go on. Ridiculous, but a useful discipline for later life. And finishing is one of the great important disciplines . . . It is the finishing of the thing that shows the quality of the craftsman.

Watch this space.

PS It's mine.

Charles Hopkinson

ON BECOMING A FAIRY GODMOTHER:
Role-Models for the Menopausal Woman

Sara Maitland

I am a 'woman of a certain age'.

I love this expression: it seems to me to be an amusing and not too insulting example of the typical euphemisms used to keep women in their places. First of all, it speaks directly to the taboo that continues to surround menopause, and therefore supports the conviction that what is not named can't hurt you. The speaker's subtext is 'I know she's menopausal but I'm not going to use *that* word.' It reveals the same shame and embarrassment as the charming habit of putting sanitary towels into a *plain brown paper bag* which, in these days of advertising, is exactly the same as pinning a button on a woman announcing in neon letters: 'I'm bleeding vaginally'. If you see a woman carrying a plain brown paper bag you know perfectly well she's menstruating (or she is unusually efficient and will be next Wednesday).

In the second place, it means the opposite of what it says – what it means is that the speaker is uncertain how old I am, into which category I fall, and how the hell to treat me. As it happens I, at least, am certain of my age – I was born in February 1950 and am therefore, at this moment of writing, forty-two and a half. The speaker, however, is not: he really thinks I am a bit too old to be wearing DMs, or skin-tight leggings, or a miniskirt, or no bra; or, alternatively, I am a bit young to be 'letting myself go', but he will very generously forgive me because, after all, I am at *that age*, and minor eccentricities or misunderstandings of my social status are only to be expected, poor thing.

In the third place, it reveals a fascinating reluctance to address the relationship between women's sexual and reproductive lives. This reluctance is, of course, extremely sensible on the part of those who wish to continue the efficient management of women's oppression: the excuse for this repression is the male 'need' to know they are the fathers of their children, the unwritten threat is that they will not support any children who are not their biological offspring. The mother's modesty and chastity are thus in the *child's* interest, and women tend to be fond of their own children quite separately from any affection they may feel towards their fathers. To acknowledge and address the sexual desire of women who can no longer bear children is to expose the whole structure; it is better to act as though they did not desire, and if they do it is peculiar, tasteless, and neurotic.

There is an unwritten law that you can have only one sexually active generation at a time. My mother-in-law had her last child when she was in the second half of her forties – this embarrassed her, she says, mainly because she *already had a grown-up daughter*. Only one of them ought to have been 'doing it' at a time. I have a teenage daughter; she is, even allowing for the bias of maternal besottedness, an exceptionally glamorous young woman (I use the word with care: glamorous originally meant witchlike – 'glamour' was both the power a witch had to deceive and delude, and the spell she cast). Last year my lovely daughter left school and went off to Paris, where she doubtless learned all sorts of things which are best learned elsewhere than under the parental eye. It is only since her return that I have started seeing that people see mc as being of that 'certain age'. I am, in terms of class and education, quite young to be the mother of so grown-up a child; many of my peer group are still having their babies, or taking their lovely daughters to primary school. Tentative conversations suggest that they are not receiving quite the same subtly coded social messages as I am; it is still appropriate for them to be 'sexy' (by which I mean, of course, that men still feel it is appropriate to find them sexually attractive) because they are still reproductive. I admit that I have internalized a great number of these implicit instructions: the handing over of eroticism to a younger generation feels both a relief and a loss, but in fairness I do not want to lumber my daughter with either projections of my desires or with seething jealousies and ownerships of hers, the two classic patterns of mothers.

Now as it happens I am not, medically, menopausal yet, but, just as there were in the few years before I was menstrual, there are signs and hints. Until about eighteen months ago I could sit down with my new diary in the first week of January and mark all the fourth Fridays in the coming year in the absolute knowledge that some time between 5 a.m. and 10 a.m. on those particular days I would start my period. (It was very convenient – and curiously, both times I stopped breastfeeding and started menstruating again, I simply took up the Friday-morning pattern even after a gap of well over a year.) This is no longer true. Luckily, in relation to laundry bills and other social niceties, there has been another change to go with this one: apart from their startling regularity, my periods were unnoticeable – I got no advance warning from my body – I would just start to bleed, bleed for five days and then stop. That was it. Now I get backaches, bad temper attacks, and cramps. These are not of a distressing intensity; indeed, I use the word 'luckily' without irony: forewarned is forearmed. However, it is a change, a new aspect of what it is to be me. I am also aware that I, who have never shaved my underarms and defended myself against considerable criticism for not doing so on the grounds of the beauty and naturalness of body hair, am giving secret consideration to what a feminist may properly do about the delicate and silky – and, fortunately, blonde – moustache that has recently begun to adorn my upper lip.

I have struggled for most of my adult life, and am still struggling, to accept the integrity of my 'self' – no, my body is not a prison, nor a showcase for, nor a tool in the service of, my True Inner Soul; but what I am, what it means to be *me*, is a single wholeness in which the body is integral. So I cannot now pretend that the 'real me' is untouched by these bodily tricks; that while my body is entering into some process of change 'I' am somehow untouched, unchanged, by this. Even if I wanted to believe this, it would be hard, because I cannot deny the social and, indeed, emotional changes too. I have bizarre regrets – why didn't I have eight children? become a contemplative nun? make lots of money? – and even more bizarre ambitions – I want to live in the country, have lots of lovers, train as a primary-school teacher, buy an aquarium, get a tattoo, be an Arctic explorer and become a grandmother (in relation to what I have said about my daughter, there is a definite *ho hum* about this one). Three years ago I hadn't even thought of any of these options for my life. Of course other changes have happened too. Perhaps this new mood has nothing to do with menopause at all. It is well-nigh impossible to tell;

but I am at least turning my mind to what feels like a new phase of my life, and the rite of passage into this new space is certainly the end of menstruation, the growing up into something new and different. But what exactly?

By and large, I think I feel more curious than frightened. On the whole I have been exceptionally lucky when it comes to biological functions. Not only have my periods been wonderfully regular, but on both occasions when I had a real longing to have a baby I was not only in a social position to realize that ambition without undue problems, but I conceived with great efficiency, bore healthy children at the end of healthy pregnancies in labours that were interesting, pleasurable and without medical intervention. Then, with great sensual delight, I lactated to the little ones' satisfaction. I found usable, appropriate and effective contraception and have therefore barely had to endure the worry about – let alone the reality of – unwanted pregnancies. I also have a total of three fillings in my teeth, and apart from having my tonsils removed when I was four I have never had a real physical illness. On the basis of past experience I do not approach menopause with the terror that medical and mythological report ought to induce in me. *They* warned me about periods, about childbirth and about the dentist, too, and *they* were wrong. I have no reason to suspect that menopause will be more horrible than interesting. Of course I may be wrong, but that's not important right now.

The point is that it is a change, and I want to prepare for it. And I don't mean yet another conversation between the convinced antis and the convinced pros about HRT. What I want to talk about is menopause more generally: about, for example, the evolutionary and socially interesting fact that menopause (unlike, as it turns out, tool-using, problem-solving, aural communication, and most of the other 'special' skills on which androcentric science has settled) is apparently unique to *Homo sapiens*. About the psychologically and politically interesting fact that although women are defined by their reproductive capacity, with the increase in the birth rate and the increase in life expectancy most women now fall outside the definition laid on them: the majority are pre- or post-menstrual.

There is a vast conspiracy of silence about menopause. It is hard to think of anything very interesting to say when to say anything at all is such an effort: 'Had any good hot flushes recently?' is not a great conversation starter. People who are gleefully ready to discuss whether a Cabinet Minister really did 'do it' in a Chelsea Strip giggle slightly nervously and decide it's time for coffee if the subject of menopause comes up.

Just in itself, this is quite odd. If menstruation is taboo because it is a place of fear and power that men need to avoid, you might expect that menopause would be a relief and a joy to everyone, admitting women to a new sphere of equality – particularly as most heterosexual men appear to be convinced that post-menopausal women could not possibly be interested in sex, and they are therefore quite safe. If what is disgusting about women is that they bleed secretly and evilly, that they go away into their own place where men may not follow them, then the certainty that a woman is not going to menstruate ought to be reassuring. The fact that they can no longer present 'their' man with some other man's children ought to mean that the controls over their 'purity' could be lifted.

Indeed, there are some societies in which this is the case:

> Where reproductivity has been regarded as somewhat impure and ceremonially disqualifying – as in Bali – the post-menopausal woman and the virgin girl work together at ceremonies in which women of childbearing age are debarred. Where modesty of speech and action is

enjoined on women, such behaviour may no longer be asked from the older woman, who may use obscene language as freely or more freely than any man.[1]

By the time her sons were mature and she was widowed, a Chinese woman was [in] . . . almost the only situation in which a woman could really shake off male domination and assume a domination over males without incurring definite social disapproval. Moreover any attempt to 'put her in her place', save in extreme cases, would probably have been socially disapproved.[2]

Fairly obviously, some of the shame around menopause is attached to the extreme negative reading of old age in our society, particularly in relation to women. While men over forty frequently become 'distinguished-looking', women simply 'go off'. They are neither sexy nor useful, and must struggle to 'grow old gracefully', which means make way for the young, glamorous, golden princess whom distinguished middle-aged men apparently want to fuck. They must struggle to learn 'resignation', that tragic pseudovirtue. Even though they may well have more than half their life ahead of them, they must learn, as quietly as possible, to 'go gentle into that good night', and never 'rage against the dying of the light'. Despite the global need for population reduction, despite men's irresponsibility towards their existing children, this disappearing trick played on women's sexuality is frequently defended as 'natural' and 'evolutionary'. Even psychoanalysts throw up their hands in despair; women at menopause move out beyond their help and good management:

Successful psychotherapy in the climacterium is made difficult because usually there is little one can offer the patient as a substitute for the fantasy gratifications.

There is a large element of real fear behind the neurotic anxiety, for reality has actually become poor in prospects, and resignation without compensation is often the only solution.[3]

Middle age – for women, though not for men – and therefore menopause, has been eliminated as a thing in itself and made merely the gateway to old age and decrepitude. As Germaine Greer[4] points out in her book about menopause, practically no research has been done to separate the symptoms of ageing from the symptoms of menopause. Obviously there is a great deal of political and cultural feminist work to be done on the negative connotations of old age, which I hope I look forward to as well, but I'm not expecting to be old for about a quarter of a century.

It is this sense that I have not one but at least two more great voyages of exploration, two whole new quests, that makes me resistant to Greer's thesis that menopause liberates one into the land of the Crone: ancient, crazed and powerful, seen passing along shadowed rural lanes at sundown and in the dawn. I do want to be Crone, the witch, Baba Ya in her little house with chicken legs; the one who teaches Gretel good sense through fear; the one who is midwife to the girl child and sole rebuker of the haughty prince; the one who has familiars from the world of the forest and speaks the language of the birds, but – although I recognize that this role needs preparation and practice – I feel I need to keep it for the next passage. I shall want to use it when I'm old. I am not imaginatively convinced that the way to combat the people who need to maintain their youth is to claim, illegitimately, my old age.

There have to be some other ways, models for me and other women looking into this foggy abyss of the unspoken to use, explore, test, adapt and reject: symbols of hope, or at least of presence, of existence. And with all due respect to Jung, archetypes and symbols – recognized patterns of meaning – are not ahistorical, transcendent, idealist absolutes. They are socially constructed. Equally, they are not abstracts, purified essences of experience or meaning; they are constructed within contexts, and these contexts are *narratives* – and, indeed, shared narratives. In fact Greer ends her book with a strong lament at the lack of – and a plea for the development of – stories about this physical and psychic passage, although, interestingly, she fails to offer any. It would be nice if women could speak their own personal stories more comfortably, without the oppressive weight of silencing, but we also need more communal stories. We need to be able to relate our menopausal selves to a whole social tradition. The frequently proposed and glorified feminist task of creating individual meanings from our own bodily experience cannot but leave us with fragmented and personalized complexes of images, rather than shared and collective patterns of meanings. Nor are there any clear indications as to how these complexes might communicate with each other within social structures.

The problem is that the taboo on menopause is very profound. It is not merely that I cannot comfortably talk about menopause at the dinner table; the menopausal woman has been banned from the tales and rituals of European culture. Even the Hebrew Scriptures, the most sexually explicit and socially grounded of our mythologies, have nothing to say about the menopausal woman: she is mentioned – 'it had ceased to be with her after the manner of women'[5] – only in the cases (Sarah, Hannah) where she is about to get pregnant after all. The Roman Catholic Church – which has made most explicit the sexual rules for our culture, and teaches, still, that the only proper use of sexuality is reproduction – is equally silent about the marital duties of those who are past childbearing. There really are no stories; and this is odd. On the whole, if a subject is socially prohibited there is a compensation in the density of its appearance in myth, folk tales or regulation.

This absence is truly interesting. I have toyed with the idea that the menopausal and the post-menopausal woman are, historically speaking, a comparatively new phenomenon; that it is the improvement in diet and reproductive control, leading to the enormously increased life expectancy of contemporary women, which has created this as a novel passage. Until the eighteenth century, and for a great deal longer in both the industrialized and the rural working classes, those women who lived so long – physically worn out by the strains of childbearing (as Adrienne Rich so movingly describes in *Of Woman Born*[6]) – moved very rapidly from being reproductive to being old: a single transition. Middle-aged women are not in the stories because they did not exist when the stories were being laid down. Old age, although it is presented as predominantly a negative state, is none the less well documented and mythologized, particularly in the Witch, though occasionally as the ancient wise-woman or hermit saint, or as the proper recipient of charity-that-will-be-rewarded.

Although this is probably an arguable thesis from a medical point of view, it is not quite satisfactory because it does not account for how many of those folk stories which have female protagonists (the Princess) are precisely about her successful seizing of the sexual initiative from the bad mother (the wicked stepmother) who wants to hold on to it – both by denying the young woman's beauty, and by endeavouring to maintain her own. Wicked stepmothers are not crones: they are not ancient women, way outside the arena of sexual attractiveness. Although Cinderella's stepmother has two ugly daughters, there is no suggestion that she herself is ugly; indeed, she manages to marry the Father despite the perfection of his first wife. Snow White's stepmother is extravagantly beautiful and physically highly active. Hera, the wife of Zeus, uses her own sexual potency as a weapon in the persecution of her stepchildren. But they are all Bad: they are women who have transgressed the rule that when your daughter comes of age you must hand over your sexuality to her. In order to secure this model without undermining the equally important message of youthful respect for one's parents as representatives of the establishment, it is necessary to dump the good mother (who passionately wanted the child, even though it meant risking her life) either by death (Cinderella, Snow White, etc.) or, more simply, by consigning her to oblivion. (The number of kings who have daughters, but apparently no wives, is quite extraordinary: the Twelve Dancing Princesses, the Goose Girl, Beauty, in *Beauty and the Beast*.) It is also necessary to fudge the question of the stepmother's precise age. Although some of them come into their second marriage with children, none of them ever produces any; jealousy for the rights of their own younger children is a surprisingly rare motif.

The women on whom all these stories focus are the Princess and the Mother – the woman who desires to be a mother, or sacrifices herself for her child. Once a woman has chosen a life partner and produced her children, she vanishes from the tales. Now, if I were a man approaching middle age, with my children grown up, there would be a great number of positive role-models available to me. There is the Good King, and with him the Good Peasant – both of whom demonstrate their wisdom in the disposition, however improbable, of their possessions and powers: they know that Honest John is deserving of the best gift, even though he is the youngest; they spot the suitable mate for their daughter, even though he is not of the princely class. There is the Mentor – King Arthur, Moses and the Greek Zeus are examples – who orders and controls the activities of a group of younger heroes. There is the Team Member – who will, like Agamemnon, sacrifice personal affection for the public good. There is the Wizard (who is also the Scholar and the Priest) who, despite long years of laborious study, is still capable of adventure and active participation and who, unlike the Witch, has both power *and* prestige. There is also God, who has the lot.

Even more important than the existence of these types is the complexity of their stories: they can be good, better or best. They can fail and get second chances. They can fail tragically or through personal weakness. They can succeed in some endeavours but not in others. They are flawed, faulty, rounded, and engaged: their stories are open to development. Whereas the stepmother, as well as being damned, is also doomed: the minute she appears, you know how she will end up – punished. Over the last few years I have been doing women's creative writing workshops based on folk tales, and a surprisingly frequent theme is the struggle to find 'excuses' for the stepmother.[7] These range from the idea that she acts in order to protect the Princess from the incestuous desires of the Father at any price (the Princess is better off out of the household, or at least hidden in the back kitchen) to the suggestion that sadism gives her positive pleasure, or that she is raging against the institution of marriage, and the Princess's desire for it is a stupidity in need of punishment. The thrust of all these versions seems to me to be an attempt to give complexity and choice to the passive and predetermined narrative.

Those of us who are the mothers of daughters do indeed have a difficult task to perform releasing a daughter into adulthood and remeeting her as woman – even, it is to be hoped, as friend. But it is important to remember that (a) this task is perfectly possible; (b) it is not one of self-sacrifice. It is clearly in our own interest to do it:

Women who have over-involved relationships with their children are more likely to suffer depression in their postparental period than women who do not have such relationships. Housewives have a higher rate of depression than working women. Middle-class housewives have a higher rate of depression than working-class housewives.[8]

Thus the wicked stepmother's refusal to allow the Princess her adult womanhood is not a wild act of selfishness but a tragic act of self-damage, which perhaps changes the idea of 'punishment'. Nor, outside the self-serving regulations of the sexist family, is it clear why the way to liberate a daughter is to give away one's own adult sensuality, instead of displaying it as a delight.

I suggest that the desire to explore the inner complexities of the stepmother is not enough; and that we need to search more widely for mythopoeic models of and complex narratives about the menopausal, or post-parental, woman in order to have a framework in which to speak of our own experience and measure ourselves – positively or negatively – against them. The Witch or Crone, for example, has become, in feminist fiction, poetry and humour, an empowering image; and narratives about her, from history and cultural production, have taken on a depth and flexibility that are surprising and enchanting. Although these narratives have not yet overwhelmed the predominating fear of age and the real inadequacy of social provision, 'grey power' is a growing economic and political force and, among women, the idea of 'growing old disgracefully' has a developing appeal.[9]

Given the aforementioned absence of ourselves from the cultural texts, this search has to be crafty as well as determined, but it is made both simpler and more interesting by the fact that we need not look for anodyne Princesses, 'perfect' heroines to live happily ever after, but for complex women who have lived and learned, and have lives or stories capable of multilayered, even tragic, readings.

There is a fascinating literary task here: how many of the women characters of folk stories and mythology do we assume to be either much older or much younger than minor details of the plot actually suggest? Ancient women do not have pre-pubescent children, for example, yet Jack's mother in *Jack and the Beanstalk* is always illustrated as a sweet little old dear. Nor do very young women have adult children, but Guinevere remains pictured as the innocent child queen, although she has seen an entire second generation of knights, including her lover's son, fully grown up before she commits adultery with Lancelot. Helen of Troy, the most desirable woman in her world, with 'the face that launch'd a thousand ships,/And burned the topless towers of Ilium,' must have been at least fifty when she ran away to Troy with Paris, and caused the Trojan War.[10] The Virgin Mary is necessarily a menopausal woman at the time of the Crucifixion, though you would not guess it from the many pictures of her at the foot of the Cross, or holding her dead son in her arms.

In terms, however, of developing, or foregrounding, imaginative role-models from the existing body of material, I have to admit that my own explorations have not developed very far yet, but there are three particular areas that I am finding potentially helpful.

The first is the role of the Prophetess – or the Sibyl, Seer, or Priestess:

Deborah, a Prophetess, the wife of Lappidoth, was judging Israel at the time. She used to sit under the palm of Deborah between Ramah and Bethel in the hill country of Ephraim; and the people of Israel came up to her for judgement. She sent and summoned Barak to her . . . and said to him 'The Lord, the God of Israel commands you, "Go, gather your men . . . and I will draw out Sisera, the general of Jabin's army, to meet you by the River Kishon with his chariots and his troops; and I will give him into your hand."' Barak said to her, 'If you will go with me, I will go; but if you will not go with me, I will not go.' And she said, 'I will surely go with you; nevertheless, the road on which you are going will not lead to your glory, for the Lord will deliver Sisera into the hands of a woman.'[11]

Deborah was not only a judge, she was also a poet and composed the great – though bloodthirsty – song in honour of her friend Jael, the tent-peg activist, 'the most blessed of all tent-dwelling women', into whose hands Sisera was indeed delivered. We have no evidence of Deborah's age, but she is a married Hebrew woman who sits in the open air, outside her village, and summons high-caste men to her, and still is held in great respect, for she is allowed to 'judge Israel'. There is therefore a real probability – especially since she is described as 'wife', not 'widow' – that she is not young, that she is past childbearing. Equally, she is not old or frail, since if she were, some special comment on Barak's requirement that she should accompany him into battle must have been made. She is the menopausal woman of religious authority, who can speak in judgement. (In Hebrew culture the role of prophecy was always as much about moral or political discernment, judgement, as it was about telling the future.)

We do know, historically, that the Delphic Sibyl was selected from women of about fifty. The Delphic Sibyl sat on a tripod in the cave and received her prophecies in a trance condition; these utterances, which were recorded manually by her attendant priests, were always spoken in verse, and were treated with the greatest seriousness, even when they were superficially entirely incomprehensible.

The Greek prophetic tradition was far closer to that of the medium or shaman than the Hebrew tradition, but points of similarity remain. These are 'mature' women of moral probity and respect who have forged a direct connection between secret knowledge and social action: neither cloistered virgins, nor deranged 'hysterics'. The tendency to think of women who have spiritual power as infantilized virgins is very much a part of our Christian inheritance, but should be resisted: Teresa of Avila, to take a historical example, did not begin her mystical and political life until she was over forty, and well honed by physical suffering and devastating self-knowledge. There is an interesting – and usable – pattern of images around the Prophetess: her political or social interventions, based on authoritative knowledge gained elsewhere; the ability, at the climacterium, to bring the traditionally private 'spirituality' of women into the public arena; and the close linking of her work with poetic self-expression. Given the deep terror among women of madness and loss of control at menopause,[12] the idea that there are these sorts of positive gains to be made out of the experience has a particular importance.

The second set of stories revolve around virgin goddesses of a particular type: not the huntress virgins like Artemis, whose virginity is an escape from men into the world of women – the radical feminist goddesses! – but the goddesses whose virginity is a sign not of the repudiation of sexuality but of autonomy. Athena, the Greek goddess of wisdom, war and the liberal arts, is perhaps the most obvious example. Athena has always had rather a bad press within feminism, based on the erroneous belief that she had no mother, but sprang fully grown from Zeus's head – the archetype of the male-identified woman. In fact Athena's mother was Metis, a daughter of the older sea god Oceanus, famous for her wisdom. Once Zeus discovered that she was pregnant, he ate her in the fear that any child of hers would grow up to be greater and cleverer than he was. The continued development of the foetal Athena despite Zeus's malevolent scheming suggests not that Athena was father-fixated, but that Zeus's fears were well founded. Later she fought off Poseidon's attempted rape, and further confounded him by winning the competition to be the titular deity of Athens. While he produced a horse as a gift to humanity, she produced the olive – providing both food and a symbol of peace. Although there are stories of her jealousy of her divine prerogatives (such as the tale of Arachne's weaving), there are more tales of her 'adoption' and great kindness towards individual humans on grounds of merit or justice, rather than because they were related to her by blood. Again there is a tendency to think of her as a younger woman, but her original iconography does not suggest this; and although her beauty is manifest, it is not infantile but adult.[13]

Both the Prophetess and the powerful but benevolent Goddess are missing from Northern European folklore, although both classical and biblical sources are as deeply embedded in contemporary Western culture as the folk tales are. This is partly for a general reason: fairy stories are different in intent from high mythologies, and seldom deal with gods or grand themes; even their kings and queens deal mainly with domestic rather than international affairs, and their emotional focus is on personal life and the family. However, there is a character, quite common in this literature, who carries a healthy combination of the characteristics of both these previous types, relates closely to the concerns of the menopausal woman, and is in urgent need of rescue from mockery and diminishment: she is the fairy godmother.

In many ways, mockery is more effective than fear in disempowering strong images. Few children are genuinely free from some terror when they encounter Disney's wicked stepmother in the cartoon version of *Snow White*. They may hate the character, but they also remember and fear her. No one, on the other hand, takes the fairy godmother seriously, played always for laughs and as an image of the ludicrous older woman who has failed to notice that her charms have departed, who is foolish and bossy. For many children the most memorable part of a performance of a *Cinderella* pantomime is the metamorphosis, the transformation scene, when Cinderella and all the vermin of the kitchen are transformed into everything desirable and brilliant. Yet the power and love that bring that transformation about are disguised by making the character with the goodwill, generosity and authority to perform the magic into a figure of fun. 'Nobody loves a fairy when she's forty,' sings the fairy godmother, pathetic and overweight in her tattered tutu, forgetting the words of her spell and needing the despised Buttons to help her out.

She needs to be laughed at if the power of the menopausal woman is to be kept invisible and covered in a blanket of shame. The fairy godmother is in fact the Good Mother who has released the girl child into autonomy without abandoning her. If one returns to the older versions of the *Cinderella* story it will be seen that it is not an actual fairy godmother who transforms Cinderella's life, but her 'real' mother from the grave. In the Grimm Brothers' retelling, for instance, Cinderella plants a tree on her mother's grave, and the tree – or the birds that nest in it – bestows upon the child the equipment she needs to achieve her desires. The fairy godmother is a personalized development of this theme; around her, once she is freed from the prison of spiteful sexist giggles, cluster a complex set of stories and images.

The fairy godmother, like the Prophetess, draws her authority from the 'other world' and exercises it in the social realm. The fairy godmother has no obligations towards anyone; like the virgin goddesses she acts only out of her own generosity and may at any time choose whom she will make the recipients of her powerful and supportive assistance. We usually see her exercising this prerogative on behalf of the oppressed adolescent (the common protagonist of these stories) at the point – and not before – when they have exhausted all their own resources. But since she has the capacity to disappear at will into her own or other stories, she is not the slave of these adolescents. Indeed, there are a whole group of stories warning the listener that they may not depend upon the goodwill of such figures; honest endeavour, kindness (especially to animals and old ladies), self-help, and luck may produce this magical inter-vention; laziness, spite and greed will almost certainly alienate it, but at best it is chancy – not like the magic horn that will most certainly summon aid. The fairy godmother may not be relied on: she has other business of her own.

A godmother, unlike other adults in relation to children, enters voluntarily into friendship with them. The words 'godmother' and 'gossip' are cognate, and the history of their relationship says a great deal about the diminishment of women and the derogation of their cultural heritage:

GOSSIP sb. (GOD + sibb – kin, related)
  1. One who has contracted a spiritual affinity with another by acting as a sponsor at baptism. 2. A familiar acquaintance, friend or chum. Formerly applied to both sexes, now only to women, and *esp*. applied to a woman's female friends invited to be present at a childbirth. 3. A person, mostly a woman, of light and trifling character, *esp*. one who delights in idle talk, a newsmonger, a tattler. 4. The conversation of such a person, idle talk, trifling or groundless rumour; tittle-tattle.

> GOSSIP vb To talk idly, mostly about other people's affairs; to go about tattling.[14]

Interestingly, recent research has suggested that women have the most positive experience of childbirth if their companion is an older woman. This would not surprise the fairy godmother, though it may well upset the New Man. The relationship between the fairy godmother and the midwife is thus a suggestive one.

The fairy godmother is neither sexually aggressive nor virginal; what she does, and with whom, is simply not relevant to the story, not anyone's business; what is clear, however, is that she does not need a hero, a king, a prince, or any other man. Her power is autonomous. She likes having fun, and has a playful and creative sense of humour. Turning rats into coachmen, after all, is practical, ironic and witty: not just a *coup de théâtre* but a *coup de grâce* as well.

From this identification, women who wish to can take on many of the role-models men have: the fairy godmother can also be the Fairy Queen (Titania, and even more potent in Celtic stories); the Mentor (the fag-hag more generously described; the good teacher with whom the girl identifies); the Team Member – fairy godmothers do not always come singly (as in *Sleeping Beauty*). Moreover, they are frequently accompanied by wise animals; and even the Wizard – given the extraordinary importance of literature, particularly poetry, in the developing of contemporary women's consciousness, the poet as fairy godmother, linking her once more with the prophet and the virgin muses, is an attractive proposition. There are other stories, too, not so easily available to men: the stories of the midwife, the gossip, the sister and the friend.

These stories are not yet told, but they are there. When they are told they will provide a structure against which to focus my own story of my menopausal years, to judge my own passage; common, shared markers through what is still lonely and unmapped territory. Signs of hope to hold up against the real fears and anxieties, magical spells of knowledge to lighten the darkness. As a writer of fiction, I cannot find it anything but exciting to want to discover the inside of those waiting untold tales. As a woman, I would find it terribly helpful to know them in advance.

Notes

1. Margaret Mead, *Male and Female* (New York: Dell Publishing Co., 1970), p. 348.
2. M. J. Levy, *The Family Revolution in Modern China* (Cambridge, MA: Harvard University Press, 1948), p. 16.
3. Helene Deutsch, *The Psychology of Women* (New York: Grune & Stratton, 1944), p. 477.
4. Germaine Greer, *The Change* (London: Hamish Hamilton, 1991).
5. Genesis 18: 11.
6. Adrienne Rich, *Of Woman Born* (London: Virago, 1977).
7. An example of this sort of fiction is my own 'The Wicked Step-mother's Lament', in *A Book of Spells* (London: Michael Joseph, 1988).
8. Pauline Bart, 'Depression in Middle-Aged Women', in *Women in Sexist Society*, ed. Vivian Gornick and Barbara Moran (New York: New American Library, 1972), pp. 177–8.
9. Realist contemporary novels, like Margaret Forster's and Margaret Lawrence's, which explore positively – or at least complexly – the emotional power of the very old, seem to me a part of this re-empowerment of the Crone, along with fantasy writing and fiction for children.
10. Helen's brothers, Castor and Pollux, sailed with the Argonauts thirty-five years before the Trojan War began. All three siblings, together with Clytemnestra, were born from the rape of Leda by Zeus, which means they were the same age. Even if the brothers were only fifteen when they joined Jason's adventure, Helen would still be menopausal when she left Greece for Asia Minor.

It is interesting also that although both she and Paris had previous children, they had none together.

11. Judges 4: 4–9.

12. See, for example, Paula Weideger, *Menstruation and Menopause* (New York: Dell Publishing Co., 1975) for documentation and comment.

13. Various contemporary Christian feminists – including myself – have tried in the last few years to reinterpret the lives of some of the virgin saints along these lines, assisted by important new work on the history of sexuality and Christian ideology by, for example, Caroline Bynum and Peter Brown, in which virginity becomes a symbol of women's power, autonomy, and radical opposition to patriarchal control. This is something of an uphill struggle, given the extremely passive and saccharine presentation of these women by the churches over the centuries; it is, however, an interesting engagement.

14. *Oxford English Dictionary*.

BIOGRAPHIES

DOREEN ASSO was born in south-east England of an English mother, Spanish father. She went to work (in information services and the film industry) and, later, to marry, in Paris. She returned to England in the sixties to train in clinical psychology and did a Ph.D at the Middlesex Hospital Medical School. She embarked on a long and rewarding (continuing) academic and clinical career; she also embarked, serially, on two long and important relationships. She has no children. Her research interests are the psychological effects of a brain operation for Parkinsonism; young children's perceptions of letter reversals; and, ongoing, psychology and physiology of the menstrual cycle. Her published works include *The Real Menstrual Cycle*; *Cyclical Variations*; and papers and talks on the implications for counselling and self-help of recent findings on biological cycles. She lives in London.

DEIRDRE BAIR (born 1935) writes about contemporary culture and society, most particularly the biographies of those persons who have influenced both. She has written lives of Samuel Beckett and Simone de Beauvoir, and is completing lives of Anaïs Nin and Colette. She wrote for newspapers and magazines for ten years, and is currently an independent scholar and writer and a member of the New York Institute for the Humanities at New York University. Married for 35 years to Lavon H. Bair, she is the mother of an adult son and daughter. She divides her time between New York City and Easton, Connecticut.

SARA BANERJI was born in 1932. After the Second World War, her parents, her two sisters and two brothers emigrated to Rhodesia to farm tobacco. The family returned to England when her parents divorced. In spite of financial disarray, she had a debutante season and was presented to the Queen. She then spent four years hitchhiking round Europe. She met her Indian husband in Oxford and they went to India to live, where she exhibited her paintings and rode as a jockey. On returning to England in 1973, she gave riding lessons, taught cookery at adult education classes, and ran her own garden maintenance and design business. Her six novels include *Absolute Hush*, *Writing on Skin* and *Shining Agnes*. She and her husband have three daughters and live in Oxford.

VIRGINIA BROWNE was born in 1927 and spent her childhood in Blackheath, the North Riding of Yorkshire, West Sussex and Somerset. After Oxford University she taught English Literature at Bristol University. Later jobs included teaching at Ibadan University in Nigeria and at Hull University; being a cook-general at £2-plus-keep; and producing the book items on *Woman's Hour*. She has lived in Florence for nearly twenty years, teaching English. This she did for the first twelve years at one of the rip-off schools she mentions in her article, but since 1987 she and a partner have run their own company, INPRESA, which goes into Italian industrial and commercial concerns to teach business English to top and middle management. When she is not teaching, she reads and writes.

ELIZABETH BUCHAN was born in 1948. As a child, she lived briefly in Egypt and Nigeria and various cities in England. Educated at boarding school where she was miserable, she went on to take a degree in English and History at the University of Kent. She is the author of *Beatrix Potter: a Profile*, *Silly Limericks* and three novels, *Daughters of the Storm*, *Light of the Moon* and *Consider the*

Lily. She worked for several years at Penguin Books, and is now a part-time fiction editor for Random House; she also reviews books for the *Sunday Times*. She married in 1974, is the mother of a son and a daughter and lives in London.

JANET BURROWAY was born in Tucson, Arizona, in 1936 and educated in Phoenix and at the Universities of Arizona and Cambridge. She is the author of seven novels including *Raw Silk*, *Opening Nights* and *Cutting Stone* and has written two children's books, *The Truck on the Track* and *The Giant Jam Sandwich*. Her textbook *Writing Fiction: A Guide to Narrative Craft* is used in colleges and universities throughout the United States. During the past three years she has collaborated with a choreographer and composer on pieces for the stage, employing improvisation among dancers, musicians and writer. She has two grown sons, and lives between London and Tallahassee, Florida, where she is McKenzie Professor of English Literature and Writing at Florida State University.

RUTH FAINLIGHT was born in New York City in 1931, but has lived in England since the age of fifteen, with long stays in France and Spain. She is married to the author Alan Sillitoe. They have a son and a daughter. In 1985 and 1990 she was Poet in Residence at Vanderbilt University, Nashville, Tennessee. She wrote the libretto for Erika Fox's chamber opera, *The Dancer Hotoke*, performed as part of the Royal Opera's Garden Venture in 1991 and nominated for the 1992 Laurence Olivier Award. She is now working on a libretto based on her poem *The European Story* for the 1993 Garden Venture with the composer Geoffrey Alvarez. She has published nine collections of poems, a volume of short stories, and translations from Spanish and Portuguese. Her *Selected Poems* appeared in 1987, and *The Knot* in 1990. A new collection of poems, *This Time of Year*, is due out in the autumn of 1993, and a volume of short stories from Virago in the spring of 1994.

PENELOPE FARMER was born in Kent in 1939. After university she taught for a while then trained as a social worker, but, since the birth of her first child in 1964, she has concentrated on her writing. Her first book, published when she was nineteen, was a collection of short stories. Since then she has written several novels for children, the best known of which are *The Summer Birds*, *Charlotte Sometimes* and *A Castle of Bone*. She has written five novels for adults including *Eve: Her Story*, *Glasshouses* and *Snakes and Ladders*, and one non-fiction book, *Beginnings: Creation Myths of the World*. She is currently working on an anthology of *Twins*. She is married to a doctor and lives in London.

EVA FIGES was born in 1932 in Berlin and came to England with her family just before the outbreak of the Second World War. She went to school in London and later to London University, where she read English. Her first novel, *Equinox*, was published in 1966, and her second, *Winter Journey*, won the *Guardian* Fiction Prize in 1967. She has published ten other novels, amongst them *Ghosts*, *The Seven Ages* and *The Tenancy*, and also several non-fiction books including *Patriarchal Attitudes* which appeared in 1970 and, as a key text in the feminist movement, has never been out of print since. Eva Figes still lives in London. She is the mother of Kate and Orlando Figes.

MARGARET FORSTER was born in Carlisle in 1938. From the County High School she won an Open Scholarship to Somerville College, Oxford, where she studied History. She is the author of sixteen novels, including *Have the Men Had Enough?*, *Lady's Maid* and *The Battle for Christabel*. She has also published four works of non-fiction, including *Elizabeth Barrett Browning* and, most recently, the authorised biography of *Daphne du Maurier*. She is married to writer and broadcaster Hunter Davies and they have three children. She lives in London and the Lake District.

JOANNA GOLDSWORTHY (Editor) was born in 1941 in Redhill, Surrey, the eldest of five children. When she was ten, the family emigrated to Africa – South Africa, Southern Rhodesia, Kenya and Tanganyika – where she went to school and lived until she was twenty-three, having married at twenty. Leaving Dar-es-Salaam – and her first husband – she returned to England, where she joined the publishers, Victor Gollancz Ltd, working first as Victor Gollancz's secretary, later as an editor, for twenty-seven years. She now works part-time as an editor at Doubleday, and freelances the rest of the time. She lives in London.

PHYLLIDA LAW was born in Glasgow in 1932 and educated thereabouts and at Badminton School in Bristol. Her first job was as assistant scene painter, wardrobe assistant and play as cast at the Bristol Old Vic where she designed sets and costumes for the Western Theatre Ballet (now known as the Scottish Opera Ballet). As an actress she has played at the London Old Vic, the Bristol Old Vic, the Glasgow Citizens and the National Theatre. She has toured South America and Europe and appeared in the West End in plays by Alan Bennett, Alan Ayckbourn, John Mortimer and Michael Frayn. Her last appearance in the West End was at the London Palladium in the musical *La Cage aux Folles*. She has just finished two films for Renaissance: *Peter's Friends* and *Much Ado About Nothing*. She was married to the actor/director Eric Thompson who wrote and narrated the original 'Magic Roundabout'. He died in 1982. She has two daughters, the actresses Emma and Sophie Thompson. She lives in Argyll.

SHEILA MacLEOD was born in 1939 in a village on the Isle of Lewis in the Outer Hebrides, moved to England when she was five years old and to London when she was six. She was educated at Wycombe Abbey School and Somerville College, Oxford, where she read English and also started to write seriously. She was first published in 1963 with short stories in a Faber & Faber collection of new writers. Since then she has written six novels including *Axioms*, *The Snow White Soliloquies* and *The Moving Accident*, two non-fiction books, *The Art of Starvation* (Virago, 1981) and *Lawrence's Men and Women*, two television plays and some journalism. She is divorced, has two grown-up sons, and lives in East London.

SARA MAITLAND was born in 1950, brought up in Scotland, and now lives in London. Her first novel, *Daughter of Jerusalem*, won the Somerset Maugham Award in 1979. Her other novels include *Virgin Territory*, *Three Times Table* (all published by Virago), and *Home Truths*. She has also written several collections of short stories, the most recent of which is *Women Fly When Men Aren't Watching* (Virago, 1993); a book about women and Christianity, *A Map of the New Country*; and a biography of *Vesta Tilly* (Virago, 1986), star of the British music hall.

SUE O'SULLIVAN was born in 1941. She is living temporarily in Melbourne with her sweetheart, missing London's density, her boys, and friends, but revelling in the great food, wide skies and different possibilities that Australia presents. She is most involved in work around HIV and AIDS and in exploring issues of sexuality, sexual practice and feminist political activism. Her latest publications are *Positively Women: Living with AIDS*, co-edited with Kate Thomson for Sheba (1992), and *Lesbians Talk*

(Safer) Sex, co-written with Pratibha Parmar for Scarlet (1992).

URSULA OWEN was born in Oxford in 1937 and spent the first eighteen months of her life in Berlin. After reading physiology at St Hugh's College, Oxford, she spent five years working on psychiatric problems in the community. She lived in the Middle East and America during the 60s, trying to be a sculptor and teaching at the American University in Cairo. In the early 70s she worked as an editor for various publishing companies before becoming a co-founder of Virago Press in 1974 where she was Editorial Director and later Joint Managing Director. In 1991 she was appointed Cultural Policy Adviser to the Labour Party and Director of the Paul Hamlyn Fund. She is a Governor of Parliament Hill School and on the committee of the Royal Literary Fund. She is the editor of *Fathers: Reflections by Daughters* (Virago, 1983) and co-editor of *Whose Cities?* (1991). She has one daughter, Kate, and lives in London.

MOLLY PARKIN was born in Pontycymmer, South Wales, in 1932. She spent a divided childhood between this Welsh valley and the seedy suburbs of London. At the age of seventeen she won a scholarship to art school, after which she taught art at the Elephant and Castle Secondary Modern and then got involved in adult education. She married at 25, had two daughters, and was divorced at 32. She joined *Nova* in 1964 as Fashion Editor, moved to *Harper's Bazaar*, then ended up as Fashion Editor of the *Sunday Times* in 1969, where she stayed until 1972, the year in which she was awarded Fashion Editor of the Year. Her first novel was published in 1974, and she wrote a novel a year for the next nine years. She toured a one-woman show 1984–86, until she collapsed from alcoholism. She is now agony aunt for *TV Quick*, and has her own show on Radio

Wales as well as doing a lot of freelance journalism. She has returned to painting and is working on a new exhibition of portraits and landscapes. She lives in London.

KATHLEEN ROWNTREE was born in 1938 in Northumbria, and grew up in Grimsby, Lincolnshire. She was educated at Cleethorpes Girls' Grammar School and Hull University where she studied music. For the last seventeen years she has lived on the Oxfordshire/Northamptonshire borders with her husband, a writer and professor at the Open University, and their two sons. She has written five novels, *The Quiet War of Rebecca Sheldon*, *Brief Shining*, *The Directrix*, *Between Friends* and *Tell Mrs Poole I'm Sorry*. She has also contributed to *Obsessions*, a series of television monologues broadcast on BBC2.

Also of interest

TRUTH, DARE OR PROMISE
Girls Growing up in the '50s
Edited by Liz Heron

'Again and again, the writing calls up splendidly vivid images, audible voices, places and people that have the special, looming, close-up quality that belongs to childhood experience' – *Lorna Sage*

In this superb collection of autobiographical writing, first published in 1985, twelve women who grew into feminism in the 1970s look back on their childhoods. In feeling, circumstance, class and culture, their experiences were as diverse as they were keenly felt. But the two great landmarks in this post-war Britain of 'you never had it so good' – the Welfare State and the Education Act – were a common feature which gave to many of these girlhoods, so like and yet so unlike those of their mothers, a sense of possibility, of aspiration to a different future. These are intimate, personal memoirs, ordinary and impossible stories that remind us how individual lives are shaped in infinitely complex ways.

FATHERHOOD
Men Write about Fathering
Edited by Sean French

Unlike motherhood, fatherhood must always be something of an assumption and perhaps for this reason it is an idea that everyone must create for themselves. 'Paternity teaches you about the ends of life' reflects Tim Hilton, but whatever the lessons and whatever the results of the shifts in the traditional family structure, the pieces here – by poets, novelists, journalists and essayists – run the gamut of anger, sorrow, delight, resentment, frustration and love.

The emotional minefield of fathering has never been so arrestingly explored.

John Agard ● Alan Brien ● Stewart Brown
Owen Dudley Edwards ● Laurie Flynn ● Julian Henriques
Tim Hilton ● Michael Hofmann ● Alan Jenkins ● Mervyn Jones
Gabriel Josipovici ● Les Murray ● Noah Richler
Roger Scruton ● Jocelyn Targett ● Hugo Williams

FATHERS
Reflections by Daughters
Edited by Ursula Owen

Of all the shaping human relationships, the one between father and daughter is the least written about, especially from the daughter's point of view. This book is a collage of memoirs and polemic, stories and poems, describing experiences which range from the most intense loyalty and love to the dark and painful areas of paternal tyranny and incest. Every daughter and every father will recognise something of their story here: some will realise, perhaps for the first time, just how deeply this bond has affected their lives. For these writers, whose ages range from thirteen to sixty, have produced fascinating and sometimes shocking insights into what is probably the most unresolved relationship of them all.

Contributions from Anne Boston, Dinah Brooke, Angela Carter, Eileen Fairweather, Elaine Feinstein, Olivia Harris, Cora Kaplan, Doris Lessing, Melanie MacFadyean, Sara Maitland, Julia O'Faolain, Kate Owen, Grace Paley, Adrienne Rich, Rose Rider, Michele Roberts, Sheila Rowbotham, Barbara Taylor.

BALANCING ACTS
On Being a Mother
Edited by Katherine Gieve

Thirteen women explore motherhood in this eloquent and moving collection. There are recurring questions and a wide variety of responses. How do children change women's lives? Do you, must you, become another person when you have a child? How do women who care for children also look after their own needs and desires? Can we balance children and work? How much do fathers engage in parenting?

The circumstances in which these women are bringing up their children vary hugely, and many speak of society's disregard for the needs of mothers, both over practical matters and deeper needs. Remarkably candid, *Balancing Acts* tells us much about a state 'both more overwhelming and entrancing than I could have dreamed'. The contributors are Yasmin Alibhai, Gillian Darley, Helena Kennedy, Hilary Land, Rahila Gupta, Katherine Gieve, Victoria Hardie, Elizabeth Peretz, Jean Radford, Margaret Smith, Jennifer Uglow, Julia Vellacott and Elizabeth Wilson.

THE MOTHER KNOT
Jane Lazarre

'Beautifully written . . . *The Mother Knot* says the unsayable, crackling with insights . . . Jane Lazarre ventures where no mother has ever ventured except under cover of fiction. At once profoundly consoling and terrifying, her finds are universal' – *Washington Post*

In this honest and moving book Jane Lazarre explores her own experiences of motherhood – the joy of feeling her baby move inside her, the pain and wonder of giving birth, the exhaustion of caring for a demanding newborn, the transformation of her identity, and her conflicting feelings of pleasure, fear, helplessness, love and guilt. Interweaving glimpses of daily life with internal reflections, she vividly captures the first few years of motherhood, the transition from the earliest days to the moment when her child attends a creche and she is able to pursue other commitments. Always there is ambivalence: she longs for escape to regain her lost independence, but she longs just as fiercely for total immersion in her infant. Lively, often very funny, altogether absorbing, this is an intensely personal tale which also reaches out to embrace experiences that all mothers share, raising such crucial issues as shared parenting, conceptions of the self and women's work.

OF WOMAN BORN
Motherhood as Experience and Institution
Adrienne Rich

'Rich's chapter on the relationship between mothers and daughters would alone be enough to cherish her book' – *Jill Tweedie*

'A remarkable book' – *New Society*

Now a classic of our times, *Of Woman Born* is an eloquent and passionate blend of memoir and history. Drawing on anthropology, medicine, psychology, literature and her own experience, Adrienne Rich, one of America's most distinguished poets, explores the contradictory pleasures and pains of motherhood. The result is a unique and imaginative study of universal importance for all mothers, daughters, fathers and sons.

OUT THE OTHER SIDE
Contemporary Lesbian Writing
Edited by Christian McEwen and Sue O'Sullivan

In *Out the Other Side*, a collection of essays, interviews, speeches and articles, letters and journal entries, all the contributors identify as lesbian – and proudly so! – but the issues covered are by no means exclusive. There is, for example, not a single 'coming out' story. Instead the emphasis rests on the 'other side' of being out. Once a woman defines herself as lesbian, how does it affect all the other choices in her life? How does a lesbian think about sex, about families and children, about race or class or money or work, about incest or alcoholism, health or disability?

Here, more than thirty writers, half of them living in Britain, half in North America, attempt to answer these questions. Among them are: Gloria Anzaldúa, Berta Freistadt, Meiling Jin, Audre Lorde, Siegrid Nielson, Lisa Saffron, Marg Yeo, and many more. Their experiences vary tremendously. But always there is something of a shared tone, an urgency, an engagement. It is the tone of those who know their own situation well enough to reach beyond it, whose wish to describe it is also a decision to act so that ultimately, in Irena Klepfiaz's words, 'distances dissolve and differences are nourished.'

VERY HEAVEN
Looking Back at the 1960s

'Truly, it felt like Year One, when all that was holy was in the process of being profaned' – *Angela Carter*

When the Beatles hit the charts and the mini skirt hit the streets, the world changed. Or so it seemed. Twenty years on, twenty-five women look back on their lives during the decade known as the 'swinging sixties', to the challenging days of protest and pop, and the first stirrings of the Women's Liberation Movement. Their engagingly personal memoirs describe the sheer fun and excitement of those heady times as well as the euphoria – and the uncertainties – of the new freedoms, new struggles: the 'it-changed-my-life' liberation of the Pill; Barbara Castle's days as a Cabinet Minister; trying to be a Twiggy look-alike; the eruption of the underground press with *Oz* and *Ink*; Paris and Derry in 1968; Julie Christie recalling *Darling*. For many women, it was also a decade of not belonging, of outsiderness: here are Terri Quaye's and Lee Kane's accounts of being Black in Rachman's London, and, in Uganda, Yasmin Alibhai's realisation that Britain wasn't 'home'. For Michelene Wandor 'the sixties was a time when many people went to pot/except for me/I did not/. . . I yearned a lot'. These fascinating pieces, combined with Sara Maitland's perceptive and witty introduction, make *Very Heaven* a wonderful social document.

ONCE A FEMINIST
Stories of a Generation
Interviews by Michelene Wandor

Twenty years ago, the arrival of the second wave of feminism in Britain was marked by the first ever Women's Liberation Conference at Ruskin College, Oxford; women from all over the country gathered to share their exhilarations, revelations and confusions. Many were beginning to question their role in the family, at work and in society as a whole; but who led this new wave of feminism? What made these women ready to forge radical new ideas about the world? Michelene Wandor has interviewed some of the women who were at that landmark conference, and produced a series of poignant and revealing portraits of a generation of women who came to political consciousness at a crucial moment in history. How did they want to change the world? How successfully did they change their lives? What was the relationship between the public campaigner and the private being? Testimonies from Sheila Rowbotham, Juliet Mitchell and Selma James, amongst others, provide a moving and highly readable account of the lives at the heart of a movement that has affected us all.